The
Gospel of
Loneliness

The
Gospel of
Loneliness

DWIGHT LEE WOLTER

the pilgrim press

The Pilgrim Press, 1300 East 9th Street
Cleveland, Ohio 44114
thepilgrimpress.com

Published 2023.

Scripture quotations, unless otherwise noted, are from the New Revised Standard Version of the Bible, © 1989 by the Division of Christian Education of the National Council of Churches of Christ in the United States of America. Used by permission. Changes have been made for inclusivity.

Cover art: iStock.

Printed on acid-free paper.

Library of Congress Cataloging-in-Publication Data on file.
LCCN: 2023934957

ISBN 978-0-8298-0063-0 (paper)
ISBN 978-0-8298-0064-7 (ebook)

Printed in The United States of America.

Contents

1

Introduction

A priest presides at an elaborate funeral for someone's only friend, a robot. An elderly person places an ad in a major city newspaper seeking a couple willing to adopt him as their grandfather. A man in Tokyo enters a business and rents someone just to cuddle with him. He returns several times that year to rent a pet, a friend, and several relatives for the holidays.

Having a robot as your only friend may seem to be a sad and lonely situation. But honoring any meaningful relationship at its end is beautiful. Renting a relative to celebrate the holidays, or renting a friend for a walk in the park may seem desperate and pathetic. But accepting situations you cannot readily change and not allowing them to define, dominate, or isolate you is quite noble.

Seemingly lonely situations can also be humorous, inspirational, courageous, and creative. That is what is in store for you in *The Gospel of Loneliness*.

The words gospel and loneliness do not seem to belong together. However, you will see the words gospel and loneliness often in this book. You will also see the word church.

Many people, for many reasons, feel uncomfortable with church. If you are one of them, then instead of the word church substitute people, community, gathering, or whatever you prefer. I am, indeed, often speaking of the church as a people more than a building.

Gospel is loosely defined as "good news," but the good news of loneliness is hard to imagine. It once was for me as well. I do not mock or trivialize either the gospel or loneliness. I am well acquainted with both. I suspect you are as well. But I do not define loneliness as a state of depravity that requires a cure. There is much to be learned and gained from loneliness, including companionship, prophecy, solidarity, fun, and freedom. This book is a creative and positive expression of my experience of loneliness.

Loneliness has been a part of us since the dawn of creation. It is in origin stories in faith and non-faith traditions. Loneliness is present in every family and congregation, in every castle and rented room, and in every banquet hall and soup kitchen. In Hebrew and Christian scripture, God created humankind in God's own image in part, it seems, because even God was lonely.

And yet loneliness is a taboo subject. Very rarely is it specifically mentioned in the Bible. There is a saying that there are two things you should never discuss at a dinner party: politics and religion. I believe there are actually three: politics, religion, and loneliness. Mention at a dinner party that you are lonely and people may exploit, avoid, or try to cure you.

Did you ever wonder if Eve and Adam, after their banishment, were lonely for the Garden of Eden? I would have been. Were Eve and Adam lonely for their son, Abel, who was killed by his brother Cain? Was anyone on the ark, including Noah, lonely for home as they drifted on an endless sea of darkness and uncertainty? Was it out of loneliness that Jesus cried from the cross, "Why have you forsaken me?" I cannot imagine a lonelier place or a lonelier question on the lips of a lonelier person. There are other stories in the Bible and in other traditions in which loneliness is silently and stoically entwined. These stories bear witness to our own stories and help us carry our own blessings and burdens and help others to carry their loneliness.

For some people loneliness contains significant physical, mental, emotional, and spiritual components that need to be addressed with professional help. Loneliness is frequently reported as a contributing factor in domestic violence and opioid overdose. However, people do suffer needlessly from loneliness because it is stigmatized, misunderstood, pathologized, pitied, or ignored. In so doing, they miss the benefits and strengths loneliness offers.

Great Britain has an official Minister of Loneliness, but many ministers in houses of faith rarely directly address loneliness in the pulpit, the congregation, and the community. There is a town that proudly claims to be the loneliest place in America, but no church that claims to be the loneliest church in America. Loneliness is an elephant in the room, rarely directly addressed because it is often scary and unattractive.

We do not suffer from loneliness as much as we suffer with it. Are you beginning to see the dignity and beauty in someone burying their best friend, even if it is a robot? They brought ritual, remembrance, honor, and closure even if it was to a relationship with an inanimate thing. The person who placed an ad in a newspaper seeking a couple to adopt him as a grandparent was laughed at around the world. His quest did not turn out well, but at least he tried before he died, alone and without a family. His story brought openness, candor, and attention to the relationship between loneliness and aging. His story received widespread attention because it resonated with many people.

According to the person rented as a friend, the other person guiltlessly talked the most. He was lonely for someone willing to listen and interact. It was indeed a transactional relationship. So what? Both individuals had a beautiful day and were rewarded before they went their separate ways.

Loneliness is a spiritual state that can be our companion, teacher, and guide. The eradication of loneliness is not always necessary, desirable, or possible. Loneliness is not a sin, weakness, or disease.

To abolish loneliness is to abolish creativity. Without loneliness, we would not have the lessons of Isaiah about the lonely exile. We might not have the music of Beethoven, Bach, Mozart, and the Beatles had it not been for loneliness. Dorothy Day wrote *The Long Loneliness* out of a deep and personal experience with loneliness that did not disempower her soul, but that helped create a fierce spirit of commitment and community. Hildegard of Bingen wrote that without loneliness, she would not have discovered freedom through contemplation that erases the separation between the seer and the seen, and that closes the gap between an authentic and inauthentic self. Countless beautiful songs, poems, psalms, hymns, and liturgies were born of loneliness. Nelson Mandela, Martin Luther King, Jr., Mother Theresa, and many spiritual leaders of various faith and non-faith traditions wrote about loneliness and its beneficial effect on their lives.

Loneliness is fruit that should not be forbidden. It can be savored and shared by clergy, congregation, colleagues, neighbors, and friends. Some may never enter the walls of the church, but they can be attracted to a church that grieves together, celebrates together, and grows along spiritual lines together. Such a church or community can also learn how to be lonely together, and in so doing, integrate and perhaps even transcend loneliness together.

The liberated Hebrew people, living as slaves and servants under Pharoah in Egypt, were freed, but found themselves in the wilderness; some wanted to go back. Freedom can be lonely. Out of loneliness, some people return to people and places where they have been harmed and sever contact with those who tried to help them. The liminal space between tradition and transition can be lonely as people attempt to let go and hold on at the same time. Unable to go back, fearful to go forward, they stay stuck.

We do not need to discover new ways *around* loneliness. We are already adept at doing that. There are ways to journey *through* loneliness to discover what is valuable within and beyond it. We also can find humor and joy in the process. What is called for in this book is to explore and reintegrate creative loneliness into the lifeblood of our fellowship, family, and community.

Welcome to *The Gospel of Loneliness.*

2

A Very Brief History of Loneliness

No one is a stranger to loneliness, not even God.

Loneliness was present in the universe before humans and earth were formed. Whether called Creation or the Big Bang, lonely solitary objects sought the companionship of other celestial bodies in our universe, as they took shape and began to orbit around a single star, our sun. Gravity keeps these bodies from crashing into each other, or from drifting apart in the lonely vastness of space.

Moons orbit around planets. Stars, moons, and planets keep each other in balance. Staying close, but not too close, they spin and orbit, both as individual entities and as members of celestial families called galaxies. The Milky Way is one of billions of galaxies, solitary entities that together form neighborhood congregations in the universe. Look up on any cloudless night to gaze at stars light years away and you will sense beautiful, silent, celestial loneliness.

Loneliness is an integral part of time. It is in our nature to question, define, explain, and explore where we came from and why we are here. Origin stories in the ancient, sacred scripture of many faith and non-faith traditions reveal loneliness in people, culture, space, and how we measure the distance between them.

Yet the presence of loneliness in many origin stories is implied but not declared. Loneliness is simultaneously present and absent, now and then, in here and out there. The often dire consequences of loneliness are seen, felt, and heard, but not acknowledged. Loneliness is the rarely mentioned child of the Koran; Greek, Egyptian, and Hindu mythology; as well as Hebrew and Christian scripture.

In the Book of Genesis, God created earth and sky, land and sea, light and darkness, and many other things that were "good." God then created humankind in God's "own image." God created us out of dirt and breathed life into us. In the breath of God is a divine loneliness that seeks to see images of itself in others. Out of loneliness God sought companionship. Loneliness is in the DNA of God.

As inheritors of the gift of divine loneliness, humans, as do planets, orbit around each other. We are pulled by *spiritual* gravity into family, neighbor, tribe, and nation. Like planets seeking balance, humans also seek balance by venturing close, but not too close, lest we collide or spin off into the vastness of lonely space that lies both within and beyond us.

God created Adam because God was lonely and then created Eve because Adam was lonely. Then the serpent whispered to Adam and Eve about the loneliness of separation, insinuating they were incomplete without a certain knowledge. Paradise was not good enough, the serpent claimed.

Many scholars say the first sin was Eve and Adam wanting to be like God. They acquired knowledge that they were *already* like God. They were like God, in the very least, in sharing the divine attribute of loneliness.

Part of the forbidden knowledge was the immense power of humans and their divinely inspired and inherited loneliness that could be both a blessing and a curse upon the world. Loneliness can motivate us to seek blessed union with each other, as well as to dismantle and curse the unions we have sought. Like a sharp knife in a home with children, loneliness can be both a useful tool and a dangerous weapon.

Once banished from the garden for their transgression, it is easy to imagine that Eve and Adam were lonely for Eden. They may have wanted to return to a place and time when innocence, shame, and deceit were unknown, and where wholeness was all they knew. But any self, relationship, or place, including the Garden of Eden, will eventually be overgrown if abandoned or untended. Imagine lonely Eden, abandoned, silent, and unseen.

Bonded by banishment and loneliness, Adam and Eve left the garden and wandered east of Eden to the land of Nod (the Hebrew root of the verb "to wander"). They entered the Land of Wandering where they, too, created life in their own image. They named their creations Cain and Abel. The first family created the first children, creating the first murder when Cain killed his brother Abel.

We might imagine Eve and Adam were lonely for Eden. We might imagine the grieving parents lonely for their deceased child Abel. We might even imagine Cain was sometimes lonely for the companionship of his brother whom he had killed. Through stories such as this, the knowledge and experience of loneliness has been transmitted from epoch to epoch and person to person.

It seems peculiar that in the first book of the Bible, loneliness is not mentioned even though it was most certainly felt. If not deemed unworthy or trivial, perhaps loneliness was too shameful, dangerous, or sinful to disclose. How strange that temptation, deceit, blame, shame, wickedness, injustice, inequality, gender bias, and even murder were worthy of mention, but not loneliness.

The absence of loneliness is not confined to the Bible's first family. Consider Noah. Surrounded in cramped quarters by family and all of creation, Noah floated on a sea of uncertainty and expectation in a dark and watery world.

Despite being on a mission from God, it is easy to imagine that Noah experienced the loneliness of leadership. How lonely to be the only chosen and trusted commander of the ship of salvation. How lonely to witness the world flooded because of its wickedness. Although obediently responding to a higher calling, it must have been lonely knowing it would entail closing the door of the ark and denying entrance to friends, neighbors, and others clamoring to get aboard. The dutiful and faithful Noah must have been lonely, without a single solid rock on which to stand.

Noah may have believed he did not have the right to be lonely, or to talk to anyone about it, not even God, for fear that feeling loneliness betrayed God's trust placed solely in him. He may have experienced loneliness as a weakness of character that if unleashed would spread like a virus. The specter of loneliness onboard might cause people to lose confidence in their own purpose and mission, leaving them adrift in an endless sea of doubt. If they saw even a speck of loneliness in Noah, the watery flood *beneath* them could be matched by the murky flood of loneliness *within* them.

Those on board may have been profoundly grateful to be alive, but they may also have been profoundly lonely for solid ground. Like Adam and Eve, they may have been lonely for their home and garden. They may have been lonely for the sound of birds in trees and the smell of fruits and flowers.

If Adam, Eve, Cain, Noah, and others experienced loneliness, they kept it to themselves. Or perhaps spoken by oral storytellers, the scribes who penned the stories redacted it. They may have felt that stoicism, odes to flawless faith, and commendations of endurance on the ark might serve the people well, but not loneliness. As long as loneliness remains unmentionable, it creates troubling results, even for God.

In the story of Noah, God destroyed people because violent humankind disappointed and infuriated God. No longer seeing God's own image in humans, God drowned everything that had the breath of life in its nostrils. And God was lonely once again.

Noah and those with him on the ark who survived the flood must have been very lonely for the deceased loved ones they left behind. This shows us that loneliness on a rampage is as destructive as loneliness kept inside. And yet to this day, loneliness as a frequent component of self-destructive behavior and violence projected outward is rarely mentioned in church.

Genesis tells us that God "remembered Noah" and those with him on the ark. God remembered? It is difficult to imagine that anyone, especially God, could destroy the earth and not remember. I searched many Bible translations, hoping to find one where God did more than "remember." I found only one, where God "showed concern" for the survivors.

Like a potter frustrated and dissatisfied with the results of their creation, God smashed down the clay of which Adam had been formed and began anew. God would rather be lonely, it seems, than to be in the presence of those with whom God could no longer find common identity.

Here is a summation of this foundational story: God created humankind out of loneliness. God destroyed what had been created out of the loneliness of no longer seeing God's own image in humankind. It was also out of loneliness that God caused the flood of disappointment to recede and to declare it would not happen again. Loneliness, however, remains, even after we destroy the relationships we create in our own image. God reveals to scribes, prophets, poets, priests, pastors, parents, and other people that suppression, shame, and denial of loneliness can lead to violence.

It is not surprising that many people still conceptualize God as male since we still associate men with violence. Lonely men are made in the image of a lonely God. Both express their anger and frustration through violence. It was God who instigated the mass destruction of the flood. It is lonely young men, made in the image of God, who often turn to self-destruction and/or violent mass destruction. Out of loneliness, God created. And out of loneliness, God destroyed. Out of loneliness, men create, and out of loneliness, men destroy, sometimes using the Bible as inspiration.

The rainbow at the end of the flood story reminds us that it is, in part, out of loneliness that God destroys, repairs, and recreates. In the aftermath of his act of mass destruction unleased by loneliness and anger, God established a covenant that God would not destroy us again, despite disappointment in our relationship.

We failed to end God's loneliness. God failed to end ours. The loneliness we have in common with God survived the flood. None of this exploration of loneliness is specifically mentioned or directly explored in the Bible. Loneliness is not the only symptom or cause of trouble; but it is the least addressed.

The time has come to change.

The physical ark of Noah was never found but the spiritual ark of loneliness was never lost. A precedent for how to not deal with loneliness was set in ancient scripture as a cautionary tale for people to this day. Each of us, as captain of our own ark, surround ourselves with distractions to avoid loneliness within. We fear that, if released, it will drown us more surely than the great flood. But addressing loneliness directly can be a life preserver for the church.

The waters receding after the flood is not the end of the story. Once the great flood ended, Noah disembarked, built an altar, and worshipped God. Imagine the joy of seeing solid ground again! That was undoubtedly not all they could see. They could see the desolation of dead animals and furniture caught in treetops. They could see buildings, walls, and bridges washed away.

As in the Old Testament, the New Testament avoids loneliness. Jesus enters the wilderness for forty days where he fasts and is met by the "Tempter" who taunts and tempts Jesus with many things. Jesus resists. The Tempter departs. Jesus emerged from his wilderness experience stronger and better prepared to live and minister amidst the sorrow, sickness, despair, loneliness, joy, and hope in this beautiful but troubled world.

We know that Jesus experienced grief, loss, and sadness. The shortest sentence in the Bible is "Jesus wept." He wept upon hearing of the death of his friend Lazarus. Jesus also wept "tears of blood" in the Garden of Gethsemane, prior to his arrest and the events leading to his crucifixion. Grief, loss, and sadness are acceptable to the human palate. Loneliness is not.

In the Bible, Jesus seems to have never experienced loneliness. He was fully divine and fully human, but not so fully human that he was lonely. Jesus had God. Jesus had perspective. He was on a mission and aware of eternal life. The Son of God had purpose. A lonely Jesus might seem self-centered, needy, and ungrateful.

We are told we should model ourselves on Jesus. If we want to be like Jesus, then we should not be lonely. If loneliness is not mentioned in the New Testament or the Old Testament, it shouldn't be mentioned in church either, unless as a sad and temporary inconvenience that can be resolved with prayer and group activity. Go bowling. Volunteer at a soup kitchen. Keep busy. Stop feeling sorry for yourself. Get away from loneliness as soon as possible. It's un-Biblical.

Loneliness is even rarely mentioned in hymns. Take, for example, "The Old Rugged Cross" in which the cross is "stained with blood so divine." According to the lyrics, the cross is an emblem of suffering, shame, death, and divine blood. The cross is never, however, called an emblem of loneliness, even though it is difficult to imagine a lonelier place than the cross while suffocating to death and crying out, as loved ones watch, "O, God, why have you forsaken me?"

The Bible is not the only place where loneliness is present but ignored. Loneliness is conspicuously absent in many faith and non-faith traditions. In Greek mythology, Hera is the wife of Zeus, king of the gods. She is strongly associated with family, women, and children. She is also miserable and quite lonely (though the word loneliness is never used), because her husband had multiple affairs. She is married to a god and yet lonely as a widow.

In Egyptian mythology, Nun was the genderless god of the chaos of primordial waters that existed before the creation of land. Being on water with no land in sight is a lonely life. Noah would know that. Floating on a sea of uncertainly, hoping to someday set foot on solid ground, seems to be a lonely way to live.

There is a saying "it's lonely at the top." It is also lonely at the bottom. In Greek mythology, Atlas was ordered by Zeus to hold up the globe-shaped heavens on his back for eternity. If Atlas shrugged even a little, everything might spin out of control. Talk about a lonely job!

In Hindu mythology, a lotus flower grew out of the navel of Lord Vishnu, a deity also known as the Preserver. Brahma, the Creator, sat on the lotus flower. Out of loneliness, Brahma split into two parts creating male and female, and from them came all beings. Here we have yet another faith tradition in which a god is inherently lonely. Perhaps the act of creation creates loneliness. Or maybe loneliness generates the urge to create. Either way, creativity, creation, and loneliness seem intrinsically related.

In addition to alternatives to violence projects taught at some wonderful churches, we can teach alternatives to loneliness. Woe to us if we simply suppress or ignore *violence*. Violence can be transformed into peace. Woe to us if we simply suppress or ignore *loneliness*. Loneliness can be transformed into creativity, compassion, and community. Like God, the first artist, whose first impulse is to create, we share a predisposition to creative loneliness. If we can teach alternatives to violence we can teach alternatives to loneliness. Creativity is key to the transformation of many things, including violence and loneliness, into positive expressions of what is often considered to be negativity.

The goal of this book, therefore, is not to abolish loneliness. It is here to stay. If loneliness is denied or ignored from the pulpit and the pew, we fail to meet the basic reality of our humanity in which we are lonely together.

We have learned how to grieve together, celebrate together, and to grow along spiritual lines together. This means we can learn how to be lonely together. If we do, we will become stronger and more resilient. We will be better equipped to minister to each other and become more complete.

3

Four Words Defined

Gospel

Many people define gospel as "good news." Some wonder why the word gospel is in the title *The Gospel of Loneliness*. They cannot imagine there is any good news in loneliness. Some believe gospel pertains only to the birth, death, and resurrection of Jesus.

Other people associate the word gospel with gospel music that has deep roots in spirituals sung by enslaved people in the United States. The spread of gospel music is often associated with Thomas A. Dorsey and other African-American composers, performers, and churches.

The musical *Godspell* took its name from the Old English word, Godspel, that also translates as good news. *Godspell* influenced the titles of books using the word gospel including *The Gospel According to Coco Chanel*, *The Gospel of the Simpsons*, and *The Gospel of Winnie The Poo*.

The apostle Paul wrote that the gospel is about faith, but he also wrote about the Gospel of Peace (Ephesians 6:15). Andrew Carnegie wrote *The Gospel of Wealth* about how it is incumbent on those who have been blessed with great fortune to shoulder the responsibility of generosity to the poor.

Whether you encounter good news through Broadway or Bible, through Godspell or gospel and whether you capitalize the "G" or not, it is naming and claiming (not shaming and blaming) ourselves and each other for the loneliness we experience that will enable us to witness the transformation of our homes, churches, and communities. That is *The Gospel of Loneliness*.

Loneliness

Loneliness is a sign of the powerful presence of love. If you feel lonely, it means you still have hope. But first, take a moment to consider what loneliness is and is not:

Loneliness Is Energy

The First Law of Thermodynamics states that matter and energy cannot be created or destroyed; it can only be transformed. Similarly, loneliness cannot be created or destroyed; it can only be transformed. It can be converted into anger, depression, numbness, bad health, addiction, isolation, and hopelessness. But it can also be changed into creativity, compassion, empathy, and social awareness.

Loneliness Is Powerful

Loneliness is like water. It can quench you, and you can drown in it. Loneliness can rage like a river, or be as still as a lake. You can skate across it, or fall into it. You can be baptized in it, wash with it, and drift away on it. Loneliness can boil your mind and freeze your feelings. It is a gentle rain that can become a hurricane. People try to swim upstream against loneliness, or get to the bottom of it. Others build dams to hold loneliness back, and levees to control the direction of it.

Loneliness Is Cunning

Some people are so lonely and have been for so long they don't even know they're lonely. Unaware of their loneliness, they are not motivated to do anything about it. Not hearing much about loneliness among friends, family, or even in church, they suspect that being lonely is just the way they are. Many people treat loneliness with isolation. In these ways and others, loneliness flies under the radar, undetected.

Loneliness Is Stigmatized

It is labelled, minimized, denied, pitied, rejected, medicated, misunderstood, and exploited. Even churches can discriminate against lonely people, not inviting them to outings and dinners where couples predominate. Lonely people are labelled as introverted, antisocial, reclusive, solitary loners. Consequently, people will more readily admit to being angry, envious, sad, aggressive, stingy, lazy, or loud than they will admit to being lonely. Lonely people may, knowingly or not, internalize the stigma and fault themselves.

Loneliness Is Considered a Deficit

Many people believe that loneliness renders them less valuable or attractive than others. To compensate for their supposed deficiency, they try to eject, subdue, ignore, and deny loneliness. They may get angry at it, drink over it, slouch under the weight of it; fear it; forget about it; roll around in it; and kick it off their boots like mud. They try to coopt its power by making it seem that their loneliness is part of their persona. They become the Lonesome Cowboy, the Wounded Woman, the Starving Artist, the Suffering Servant. They overcompensate for the loneliness by trying to turn it into an attribute, a positive characteristic.

Loneliness Makes People Uncomfortable
Restaurants rarely place a single person at a table near the front door. Tour companies do not advertise vacations with photos of people sitting alone at the edge of a dancefloor. Lonely people make non-lonely people sad. Lonely people can seem exhausting to be around.

Loneliness Is a Portal
When people survive loneliness and it has not numbed them into indifference or defeat, they may come to admit, accept, release, and be transformed by it. It can be a doorway through which people pass to become more resilient and compassionate.

Loneliness Is Not Mental Illness
Some lonely people with medical conditions could benefit from professional help, including medication. We are all somewhat physically, mentally, emotionally, or spiritually ill. However, lonely people in church or home are not our patients. And loneliness is not mental illness.

Loneliness Is Not a Feeling
If you look at dictionary definitions of loneliness, you will read of loneliness being a feeling of deep sadness caused by having no friends or company. But if loneliness is having no friends or company, we would not know being lonely in a crowd, a marriage, or some other relationship. Loneliness provokes feelings but is not defined by them.

Loneliness Is Not a Situation
If loneliness was just a situation, then loneliness could be remedied by moving on to another job, house, city, watering hole,

health regimen, church, or partner. But we have all heard about some lonely person packing their bags and moving on, and then unpacking loneliness that somehow came along to their new situation. Loneliness may provoke the desire to change a situation, but it is not defined by changing a situation.

Loneliness Is Not a Disease

Loneliness is not a tumor. We can try to shrink it. We can try to develop a vaccine against it and stomp it out in our lifetime like we did with polio but we will fail. Loneliness is a part of our human identity, not a disease.

Loneliness Is Not Fuel for Blame

You may feel lonely because your lover left you. You might angrily shake your finger of blame at someone. But blame often places the reason for loneliness upon the wrong person or circumstance.

While loneliness may be triggered by people and circumstances, loneliness is in you, not in circumstances or people that come your way. You may be powerless over circumstances. But you are not powerless over your reactions and responses. Perceptions may change. Someday you may be grateful to the person or circumstance you once blamed when you were led by loneliness to someone or something better.

Loneliness Is Not About Shame

Loneliness may be your chosen response to a poor choice. Making a mistake, however, does not mean you are a mistake. Shame is toxic. Sermons, books, and podcasts about basking in God's love without acknowledging the reality of loneliness may cut even deeper into the souls of already lonely people.

Punishing yourself with loneliness will not end shame. Climbing on a cross of loneliness is not atonement for sin. People hiding their loneliness from each other will not heal a wounded soul. Freeing loneliness from judgement and shame may lead you to becoming a source of health, hope, and healing for others.

Loneliness Is Not Going Away

The COVID-19 pandemic brought loneliness out into the open and revealed similarities between COVID-19 and loneliness. At its onset, we declared a war on COVID-19. It was an enemy that we were going to defeat. We were told to cooperate with science, to distance ourselves from each other, and to not give this entity called COVID-19 an opening to take us down. Now we are told to learn to live with the disease because it is not going away. Loneliness is also not going away. The good news is that from loneliness comes resilience. From weakness emerges newfound strength, awareness, acceptance, and action.

Loneliness Is Not Procrastination

Waiting for the perfect moment to address loneliness is not a good idea. Some people, including, perhaps, your pastor, are lonely. Loneliness casts many people into darkness. We must confront loneliness now rather than later before it takes a toll on us.

Isolation

Loneliness is loneliness. Isolation is isolation. They sometimes intersect but they are not the same. Loneliness is not synonymous for isolation.

Isolation can be involuntary. A judge could incarcerate me and make me isolated. But a judge could not incarcerate me and make me lonely. Loneliness is often an inside job. Isolation is often not. Isolation can also be voluntary. If I home test myself for COVID-19 and learn that I am positive, I could isolate myself. But I could not isolate myself from loneliness. There is no home test kit for loneliness or isolation.

Many lonely people feel they did not choose loneliness. It chose them. Some people feel they did not choose isolation; but that isolation was chosen for them by organizations, institutions, and systemic injustices that isolate them from the dominant culture. They did not consciously choose to be lonely or isolated.

However, some lonely people feel uncomfortable around others, so they isolate themselves. They may crave human contact but don't know how to achieve it. Isolation feels like their natural state of being. Their isolation is their fortress and loneliness is their moat. In their isolation, the pain of loneliness may be absent, but so too is their sense of joy.

Solitude

> "Our language . . . has created the word loneliness to express the pain of being alone. And it has created the word solitude to express the glory of being alone." — Paul Tillich[1]

Solitary confinement in prison is a misnomer. It has nothing to do with solitude. It should be called isolation incarceration. Solitude is inappropriate to describe what, by many accounts, is the brutal treatment of people, many mentally ill, who are ill-equipped to endure a long time of being forced to be completely alone. Forced solitude is not solitude.

Voluntary solitude has been a part of many faith traditions for many centuries for many reasons. Here are some definitions of solitude:

- ❈ A time of separation voluntarily spent in prayer, contemplation, and reflection.

- ❈ Terms applied to persons who are committed to solitude include hermit, recluse, and solitudinarian.

- ❈ Isolation is a time of being alone, and solitude is a time of being alone with God.

❀ A constructive way to achieve spiritual engagement with oneself.

❀ A state of being with oneself that may or may not include loneliness.

❀ Some siblings of solitude are silence and surrender.

❀ In solitude you discover you are never alone.

❀ Solitude is not for everyone, although, at time, loneliness is.

4

All the Lonely People

Wherever people are, loneliness is there also. There are no exceptions. Here are some of the lonely people among us:

People Lonely for Things Other than People

People are not always lonely for people. They may be lonely for a place they once called home, or a sense of purpose, hope, and health they had when they were younger. Or they may be lonely for a God they once believed in but whom they now believe no longer exists.

It reminds me that we are all born alone and die alone. No one can be born for us and no one can die for us. In our death as in our birth, we are alone. And strangely, we spend most of the time between these two events trying not to be lonely; yet lonely we sometimes or always are.

Lonely People Falling In and Out of Love

Loneliness can be a habit. We may make fledgling forays into consecutive relationships hoping that each time things will be different. We imbibe the sweet wine of intimate companionship. We throw back a shot of romance. We settle for less than top shelf. We try again and again with new ones or with the same one who, we convince ourselves, contains the missing pieces in us and that together we will somehow, someday be whole.

Sometimes we return to the river that we have been told is clearer now. The muck has settled or departed. The thrill of doing the same thing over and over again and expecting different results is crazy-making. Loneliness can be an intoxicating aphrodisiac. Here is a poem I wrote about this:

I bought two glasses of wine

But there is only one of

me here to drink it

and so my

s

w

e

e

t

come home

We get high on love. Then comes the inevitable hangover only another bender can eliminate. The problem is, unless we change, the relationship seldom does.

Lonely People Who Have Lost a Child

A sculpture of a child angel stood at one of the corners of our swimming pool. It was made of molded cement, not chiseled marble. No one marveled at its beauty. But the child angel dutifully stood, wings unfurled, hands folded in prayer, watching over Maya and Casey, my young children, as they swam and played.

Maya was running around the pool one day, as I always told her not to, and as she always did anyway. She accidentally knocked the angel over and broke one of its wings off. After kneeling next to it, she held the wing up to the place from where it had broken off, as if it could be magically restored. She looked to me, expecting anger. It was not anger that I felt. It was dread.

A moment before, an angel with two wings watched over two children. A moment later, one wing had been severed. I quickly admonished myself, as I often do when unwelcome visions appear to me and I try to push them away. I consoled Maya as she comforted the angel with the missing wing.

A month later Maya was killed in a fiery car crash at the age of six. Casey, her ten-year-old brother, angel child of the wing not missing, was also in the car and severely injured, but survived. For months, I watched the one-winged, molded cement child angel watch over my remaining young child as he swam in the pool, often alone, sometimes with me.

One night as Casey slept, I was sick of feeling sickened by the cement angel constant reminder of the crash. I got out of bed and smashed off the other wing with a hammer. I was done with cement angelic guardian replicas of grace prayerfully not protecting my innocent children. Museums may exhibit an ancient headless statue and a priceless palace gargoyle with a missing nose. But an inexpensive one-winged cement angel was pure pain to me.

Time has flown. My daughter, Maya, is six forever. My son, Casey, grows older each day. One child was taken; one was spared. A daughter lost her life. A son and father lost their wings. Part of Maya is still alive, though departed. Part of Casey is departed, though still alive. Casey is now grown and is doing well. He never talks about his sister.

The comfortable house in which my son and I now live does not have a pool, but it does have a bathtub, which we almost never use. The angel with the missing wings is still with us, and it stands guard over the bathtub. I see the angel each morning when I enter the shower, and once again when I emerge, cleansed in the waters of loneliness for what is lost; cleansed in the waters of grief for what is dying; and cleansed in the waters of hope for what still lives.

Everything living is dying. Everything dying is alive. An angel with missing wings is still an angel. A father with a missing child is still a father. A brother with a missing sister is still a brother. Violence inflicted upon an angel made of cement or of flesh does not diminish its holiness. Rage and fear can be forms of prayer. Mercy is everywhere. And in loneliness, more so than in anger or fear, I often feel the still living love my departed child and I still share.

I can swear that the child angel with missing wings, and hands forever folded in prayer, sometimes rises from the floor; uplifted by wings that cannot be destroyed. When, on unpredictable occasions, her missing wings flap, my hair blows ever so slightly back, and I am transported to a place where the pool is clean and cool, to a place where the syncopated laughter of two children can still be heard, to a place where everything is broken and in its brokenness everything remains intact. Forever.

Lonely Pandemic People

"Turn to me and be gracious to me, for I am lonely and afflicted."
— Psalm 25:16

COVID-19 brought the specter of loneliness into every body, home, community, institution, fellowship, and congregation. COVID-19 did not create loneliness, it merely magnified and exacerbated it.

Like loneliness, the presence of COVID-19 was at first denied and minimized. People who tried to discuss and explore COVID-19 openly and immediately were called overly dramatic or even paranoid. Like loneliness, many people thought COVID-19 needed to be fought, controlled, treated, eliminated, or just allowed to run its natural course. It caused people to avoid other people in self-imposed reclusiveness, quarantine, and exile. Like loneliness, COVID-19 caused much illness and death, and people couldn't wait to see it in the rearview mirror.

The Lonely Bodies of Lonely People

Someone recently told me that, during the pandemic, she didn't realize how not only her spirit and mind were lonely. Her body was also lonely because it was never touched.

Loneliness in the body is associated with cognitive decline, stroke, obesity, coronary heart disease, and addiction. It affects our genes and immune system.[2] Loneliness is related to a region of the brain known as the Dorsal Raphe Nucleus (DRN), best known for its link to depression.[3] Loneliness is also associated with increased levels of cortisol, a major stress hormone, that may result in high blood pressure and affect the production of white blood cells, which hinders the immune system's ability to fight infections.[4] There has been research linking blindness and loneliness; obesity and loneliness; genetic predisposition to loneliness; physical trauma and loneliness.

Lonely People in Committed Relationships

People envision marriage or a long-term committed relationship as an end to loneliness. However, the presence of loneliness in marriage or long-term committed relationships is not uncommon. Loneliness can almost feel like a third partner in the relationship. Embarrassed and ashamed about feeling lonely in marriage, it may cause people to keep it a secret, even from themselves.

The actor Robin Williams said, "I used to think the worst thing in life was to end up all alone. It's not. The worst thing in life is to end up with people who make you feel alone." Kahlil Gibran wrote in *The Prophet*, "Let there be gaps in your togetherness." For some couples, the gaps in their togetherness had become a chasm.

Lonely married people may engage in compensatory activities like shopping, drinking, church groups, social organizations, and health clubs. These activities may have many rewards. But if they mask loneliness, they may also have other consequences. Up to forty percent of married people have affairs.

Sometimes people become aware of their loneliness when their children grow and leave home. Their empty nest is empty not only of children, but of intimacy with each other. Others may become physically ill. The lack of support they receive from their partner makes denying loneliness more difficult. Some marry young and assume that everyone lives in emotional and spiritual loneliness.

Lonely Women

Many women tell me they believe men are generally lonelier than women. They say men are more solitary and can be lonely and not even know it. Women are more relational. So if they are lonely, they know it sooner and are more likely to do something about it. Women more readily seek company and conversation with other women friends, colleagues, neighbors, or in places such as church.

I do not know of a single church that would still be functioning if it were not for women. For more than twenty-five years, I have preached in many states, almost always to a congregation or group comprised of about two-thirds women.

And yet, seventy percent of the calls to The Silver Line (a hotline for elderly people in Britain) are from women. If men are lonelier than women, why do women call a hotline far more often? Perhaps it is because women often live longer than men. The older you are, you have had more time to make the call. Some researchers believe hormonal change is a factor in the loneliness of women. None of this means that women are necessarily lonely for men.

Lonely Men

Many men insist they are basically self-sufficient and have less need to talk to or seek the advice of anyone. In the churches I have pastored, visited, and studied, the groups designated for men are smaller and less vocal than groups designated for women. Addiction support groups, however, are comprised of a majority of men. Alcoholics Anonymous, for example, is about two-thirds men and one-third women.[5]

Obviously, not all lonely men are alcoholics. There are more than three hundred members of what is called a "Men's Shed" throughout England, Scotland, and Ireland that brings men together through woodworking shops. It seems that as men create wooden objects, they also develop relationships. An admittedly gender-based generalization is that women often relate to each other face-to-face while men do so shoulder-to-shoulder. This means that men bond and mitigate loneliness with a "third party" in their relationship, such as sports, fishing, or in this case, woodworking.

The National Public Radio show *Hidden Brain* postulated that school-age boys establish several friendships but have difficulty holding on to friendships as they age. The suspected reason is that while all people have great capacity for social relationships, men increasingly receive messages that needing others is a sign of weakness and unmanliness.

Lonely Queer People

Among a group of friends, you make a comment about someone named Chris. All the other friends don't know which Chris you are talking about so you say, "You know, gay Chris." That may not have been said to hurt Chris; but it does hurt Chris. At least that is what my friend Chris told me when he recounted what has occurred countless times in his life. Chris knows the pain he felt was not intentionally inflicted by the group. He is aware that the name, Chris, is what is often called an androgynous name. He told me that part of his pain is because being labeled deepens his sense of separation. It reminds Chris he is perceived as different. This pain could be mitigated by describing him with other attributes such as, "Chris the insurance agent" or "Bill's husband, Chris."

Avoiding the misuse of gender pronouns might help. If I am, for example, the co-host of a Zoom event and someone raises their hand, I could easily say to the host, if the host does not see the raised hand, "Chris has their hand up" rather than "Chris has her hand up" and thus avoid misgendering them. That is not a huge change for me to make. Out of respect, I will identify them with the pronouns they prefer.

This is not a book about gender pronouns; but it is in part about becoming mindful of some of the ways in which we may unintentionally nudge people further into loneliness and isolation.

Infant Loneliness

An infant does not know its mother is a separate being until about six or seven months of age. When an infant is cuddled and nursed, the child often but not always (wouldn't it be nice) drifts off in peaceful slumber. The blissful look of an infant in this state of contentment is one no parent or caregiver forgets.

However, the moment the child is laid down on a mattress for the night, look out! It cries and trembles. Why? Perhaps it misses the heartbeat of its mother or other caregiver. A warm body is certainly preferable to a cold mattress. Perhaps it has gas pains from the feeding. Maybe its diaper is wet. We try to figure out the cause of discomfort and quickly eliminate it.

If an infant does not know it is a separate being from its mother, the infant may be crying and trembling because it is lonely. The child can't, however, be lonely for its mother, because it does not know that it is a separate being from its *mother*. The infant is lonely for missing a part of *itself*.

My daughter gave birth to twins: a girl, Sophia, and a boy, Oliver. At birth, Oliver was suspected of having a heart problem and was taken directly to neonatal intensive care. My daughter and her daughter were soon released from the hospital and went home with my son-in-law. Oliver was released several days later.

Everything worked out well for the entire family. My twin grandchildren are somewhat different. Oliver is highly sensitive. He easily bursts into tears. He needs and receives a lot of attention. Sophia is calmer, more centered, and less in need of emotional reassurance and physical proximity. Gratefully, both are healthy, loved, and thriving children.

My son-in-law believes the difference between the twins is due, in part, to Oliver's at-birth separation from his mother. My daughter doesn't see it that way. My suspicions are also neither right nor wrong. Both and neither could be true. The point is to keep an open mind and allow for the possibility that people can be born with inclinations toward loneliness that can be magnified by our earliest experiences.

This is one example of how even infants can be lonely. Perhaps, as I suspect, loneliness is in the DNA of humankind. Oliver had an earlier and stronger opportunity to manifest it than did his sister.

Youthful Loneliness

Loneliness is increasing among teenagers and young adults. Suicides among fifteen to twenty-four year-olds continue to rise. A national survey of 20,000 adults, using the UCLA Loneliness Scale, stated "the younger generation was lonelier than the older generations."

Almost half of Generation Z (born between the mid-1990s and early 2,000s); Millennials (just a little older than Gen. Z); and Baby Boomers reported being lonely.[6] Not surprisingly, research suggests social media and the large amount of time spent staring at screens may cause a rise in suicide, depression, and loneliness among American adolescents.

Elderly Loneliness

Loneliness among our aging population is expected to become even more pronounced as the Baby Boomer generation ages. For many people in this age group, their children are grown and gone from the family home, there is decreasing physical mobility, and increasing health issues lead to social isolation after retirement. Several elderly people in the churches I have served told me they read obituaries before front page news, feel invisible in a youth-oriented society, and have little savvy with technology, which intensifies isolation and loneliness.

This is not only an American problem. Many individuals and organizations report a global pandemic of loneliness in the Far East, isolated geographical areas, and elsewhere. In Britain and the United States, about one-third of people over 65 live alone.[7] While living alone does not necessarily create loneliness, it does provide an incubator for it.

Mounting evidence links loneliness to physical illness and cognitive decline. This situation is exacerbated by elderly people denying they feel lonely. The word lonely carries a negative connotation. The unspoken stigma of loneliness is evident when elderly people exhibit loneliness but won't even say the word, whether or not they are aware that they are lonely. They may say things like "I am a private person" rather than admitting they are lonely.

Lonely People Celebrating their Birthday Alone

Many years ago came another of my birthdays undramatically wedged between Christmas and New Year's Eve, between the birthday of Jesus and the birthday of Father Time.

I knew I was going to be alone that year. I thought I would go to a movie. No one in the theatre would know it was my birthday and I was there by my lonely self. It is not like I would be wearing a party hat or the scarlet letter L attached to my jacket to identify me as lonely. I decided I did not want to sit in a dark theatre, alone, on my birthday.

I went to a bakery instead, on a whim, and had "Happy Birthday Dwight!" written on a small, beautiful cake. The smiling clerk asked, "Who is Dwight?" as she squeezed blue icing out of the piping bag and carefully wrote the name in cursive letters. "Dwight is a friend of mine," I truthfully replied.

I brought the cake home in a white cardboard box tied shut with blue string and made myself dinner. A couple of hours later, I stuck one candle in the cake, lit it, dimmed the kitchen lights, and sang "Happy Birthday" to myself. I slowly ate a single slice and savored each bite. It felt like communion. I reflected on many of the blessings and curses since my last birthday. I thanked God for another year of life.

But guess what? That was the most pathetic birthday of my entire life! I will never... I repeat... never do that again! As I enacted my birthday ritual, I was fully aware that it was a sad and lonely experience. I admit I sang softly, just in case the neighbors in my Manhattan apartment building would hear.

I immediately knew that by eating a piece of birthday cake with one candle in it and singing a song of wishes for happiness to myself, I was striking a blow against an evil ogre empire telling me that there must be something wrong with me if I am alone on my birthday.

There is absolutely nothing *wrong* with being alone and lonely on a birthday, or any other day for that matter. There is actually something very *right* about a bakery writing my name on a cake, rather than allowing my mind to write an L for lonely on my soul. There is something right about me if I can muster the internal fortitude to honor myself on my birthday when I am feeling down. There is something right about me if I bowl alone, dance by myself, or seek solace in the company of the ducks and birds on a pier at an abandoned marina rather than sitting alone at home.

It is harsh judgements about loneliness, not loneliness itself, that cause the most pain. Any expression of gratitude for life, even one as simple as blowing out a single candle on a small cake, is a cause for celebration! Happy Birthday to me, indeed!

Lonely People Who Marry Themselves

> "You must understand this, that in the last days, distressing times will come. For people will be lovers of themselves . . ." — 2 Timothy 3:1

> "With This Ring I Me Wed"

Before entering a committed relationship with another person, learn to have a committed relationship with yourself. If you do not have a solid relationship with yourself, the chances that you will find someone to make you "feel complete" and less lonely are greatly diminished.

One of the creative solutions to the stigma of loneliness is to resist the dictates of society that if you are not part of a couple, you are less than a whole person. Out of a desire to have a committed relationship with themselves, and out of fatigue over waiting for what seems like forever for the right person to come along, some people marry themselves. Marrying yourself is called sologamy.

To avoid loneliness, people may flee into a mediocre relationship and end up feeling even more lonely. This begins a cycle of serial monogamy, going from one hopeful prospect to another, trying to discover what is missing.

My experience is that love is not found in a person. The love in me may manifest in another person but it is not the result of another person. It results from an ability and willingness to love, which is itself a result of having been loved. If you do not have an imprint of love in your soul, you cannot recognize and internalize it. If you learn to love yourself, you are better able to love others.

A sologamist self-marries as a symbol of their inner commitment to their self and, perhaps, to God. The Bible says that God is love; therefore love, not marriage, is the end of loneliness. Marrying yourself is, at the very least, enacting a creative and committed way of climbing out of the box of loneliness that society often says is the ultimate end to not being in a relationship.

You can purchase a self-wedding ring and vows for self-marriage online. You can buy a dress or tux, a bouquet, and invite friends to watch you walk down the aisle by yourself where no one is waiting to receive you. Then you can have a reception and invite your friends to your self-marriage before going on a honeymoon alone.

This may sound like a silly stunt. But many people seem (or even claim) to be married to their job. Athletes are faithfully devoted to their own athleticism. Artists deeply love their work and their family may feel neglected. In some religious rites, people take vows of "marriage" to God.

Lonely People Living Alone

"I lie awake; I am like a lonely bird on the housetop."
— Psalm 102:7

Between 1973 and 2011, the number of people living alone in England and Wales doubled. In the same period in America, it tripled. A popular saying attributed to many people over many years is: "If you are lonely when you are alone, you are in bad company."

The implicit thought is that if you get your act together then you won't be lonely. The problem is linking loneliness with being bad, deficient, and a lousy companion for yourself and others. There are benefits to living alone. Some people like it, whether lonely or not.

Loneliness of Addiction

"As we became subjects of King Alcohol . . . the chilling vapor that is loneliness settled down." — The AA Big Book

Some people drink because they are lonely. Others get sober and discover they are lonely.

One friend of mine in recovery told me she sobered up to realize she was lonely for love, community, and even for herself. She drank every night, thinking it was her companion and cure for what ailed her, only to discover that alcohol was her prison guard all along. Behind the bars of addiction, she lost connection to who she was, what she valued, what she was willing to die for, and more importantly, what she was willing to live for.

After she quit drinking, she joined a church and developed relationships with other people. However, the loneliness remained. So she joined a twelve-step group and that helped. But some loneliness remained. She realized some uncomfortable things are better accepted than rejected. So she befriended her loneliness, learned what it had to teach, and channeled it into creativity.

Loneliness and Fantasy Relationships

Some of us, under the influence of loneliness, reach back in time to a former partner or spouse who touched us in a way that a casual friend or romantic dalliance cannot. We imagine reaching out to them, and them reaching back. Even if they are deceased or utterly unavailable by time, distance, or circumstance, our imagination makes all things possible. Thus begins the fantasy of reunion.

Sometimes we revisit the relationship we once had, or at least thought we had. In our fantasy, we relive every drop of our love before it evaporated. After visiting every room, dresser, and closet in the beloved one's soul, we take a bite of the apple from the garden of our imagination. Every fragment of conversation we once abandoned is completed. We take that cool summer night drive we once were too busy to take. After talking about everything we once failed to talk about, we embrace each other as often as we once refrained from doing. All of this means we'll get it right this time.

It brings immense pleasure because everything always unfolds perfectly. Comfort, familiarity, relief, and inspiration fall like manna on our somewhat parched and barren life. A flame of love suddenly appears in the ashes of a flickering soul. Out of the ashes springs a resurrected love.

Fantasies of union and reunion also bring immense pain because, no matter how innocuous they may seem, fantasies take us away from being present in our life. As we place yet another virtual log on the virtual fire of a virtual companion, we risk becoming even more lonely than before we stoked the fire of delusion.

Fantasies are the wine of poetry; the bread of love that still smell of grape and wheat and earth. They can also be the drug of loneliness: a temporary high followed by denial, withdrawal, and even more of the pain we had sought to quell or avoid. Fantasy relationships lure us further into trenches where no one can reach us, including ourselves. People who appear in fantasy relationships have the uncanny ability to neatly fit into our perceptions and expectations.

Fantasies of reviving a relationship you regret having ended may make sense. Like Humpty Dumpty, however, all the King's horses and all the Queen's men can't put the relationship back together again.

Real relationships can hurt like hell. Fantasy relationships feel like heaven. You may drape the cloak of fantasy over the cold shoulders of loneliness. But fantasies of reunion are inherently dishonest. Dreams can come true but fantasies seldom do. They can be another attempt to manipulate an outcome. If you fantasize someone being with you when you are alone then you don't feel so alone. Fantasy may temporarily throw off the hounds of reality off your path through the wilderness of self. But you eventually arrive back home, alone.

Selfless and Lonely

I got into a relationship and my partner immediately went to work on getting me to change. Change I did. Now I miss me. Who am I now?

Loving parents dedicate their lives to their children and when the children grow and move away the parents are often lonely for their children. They sometimes discover they are also lonely for themselves. In doting on others, they indulge a benign neglect of self. "Where did the children go?" is soon followed by "Where did I go? Who am I now?" Does being a parent, child, employee, deacon, friend, neighbor, and constituent define me?

The emptiness and loneliness for something *outside* of yourself is compounded with an emptiness and loneliness for something *inside* of yourself. Over the years, my-self can become fused with your-self.

Some people orbit their partner like a satellite orbits a planet. If, however, one partner is dislodged from their orbit, the purpose of the other partner is called into question. When one person goes away, for whatever reason, their partner can spin off into the vast space of deep loneliness. The same can be true when one's beloved church changes or closes.

Self-Absorbed and Lonely

Few care to admit it, but many of us are lonely because we are self-absorbed and selfish. Fearing the vulnerability in relationships, we don't want to let our guard down and allow ourselves to be open. We also don't want to be lonely. Ironically, if we refuse to allow ourselves to become vulnerable to others, we become vulnerable to loneliness.

Some of us want a relationship, but only on our terms. We want to be the interior decorator of our relationships. We want to call the shots, choose the colors, arrange the furniture, set the mood. Even if we want someone else to call the shots, it is still what we want. Ironically, if we always insist on getting what we want, we get what we don't want: loneliness.

I have known several single mothers who remained single because they did not want to share authority, control, and decision-making concerning their child. Some of them are willing to pay any price to remain in control, even if the price is having sole custody of loneliness.

Incarceration and Loneliness

As you may have experienced or imagined; incarceration is often akin to being incarcerated by loneliness. Incarcerated persons are lonely for people, places, and things they left behind. They experience loneliness, even in tight quarters with other prisoners that may result in further difficulties such as depression, violence, substance use disorder, and anxiety.

Lonely Only Child

Is being an only child a curse, a blessing, or a little of each? Some people, as the only child, were well-loved and precious in the eyes of their caregivers, but they were the only child nonetheless.

Some people *choose* to have only one child. Others are *able* to have only one child. Due to their child having no siblings, parents and caregivers of only children often scramble to arrange playdates. Sunday schools welcome only children into the group and teach them how to coexist with other children.

Some claim the only child can better learn how to be self-sufficient and alone without being lonely. Others believe only children can become lonely, isolated, trapped in their thinking; talking primarily to themselves, living in imaginary relationships, and lacking the ability to modify their behavior that comes with living with a sibling. The only child, it seems, has benefits and disadvantages. They are not, however, destined to be handcuffed to the mast of loneliness as their ship lists aimlessly in lonely darkness for the duration of their childhood.

A single mother with one young child told me that her child's stuffed animals were her siblings, friends, and children. One night she slowly and quietly opened the door to her daughter's room, just to check in on her, and saw her lying on the floor! She thought her daughter had fallen out of bed, but she was sleeping comfortably on the floor, in her pajamas, with a pillow under her head and a smile on her face.

The mother saw her daughter's bed had a row of stuffed animals next to each other stretching from one side of the bed to the other. Each of them was neatly tucked-in with the sheet up to their chin. The mother jokingly said she thought she heard one of them snoring! Her daughter apparently decided to sleep on the floor because after putting all of her stuffed animals to bed there was no room in the bed for her.

It is the power of love that drives someone to give up their comfort and sleep on the floor so others may have a place of contented rest. It is an intuitive understanding of personal sacrifice for love of others that children often express through stuffed animals.

Only children are never truly alone when they have access to their creative imagination. Some may also call it magical thinking, the presence of God, or a celestial power. I call it reality. The stuffed animals were living beings for the daughter. Although the daughter claimed she preferred siblings, just look at what beauty she created.

Misunderstood People and Loneliness

Poor Job in the Bible. He was experiencing the excruciating loneliness of "no one understands me" when his three friends show up to console him. Each one is progressively less helpful than the other. As the jazz and popular music singer and activist Nina Simone sings "Oh, Lord, please don't let me be misunderstood." It seems loneliness is as indispensable to a spiritual life as fitness is to an athlete. But loneliness and fitness involve stretching, and that can be painful. But no pain, no gain.

Loneliness is part of creation. It waits within our spiritual DNA to be triggered, released, activated, or conjured. Loneliness is like the wind that is always there. We may just notice it more when it blows too strong for those walking on ice, or too weak for those on a sailboat. In our loneliness of being misunderstood, we are in good company.

5

Scripture, Fiction, Parables, and Fables of Loneliness

"The reason I speak to them in parables is that 'seeing they do not perceive, and hearing, they do not listen, nor do they understand.'" — Matthew 13:13

"I was naked and you gave me clothing." — Matthew 25:36

The Emperor's New Loneliness

In the fable "The Emperor's New Clothes," a child stands in a crowd on the side of the street as the naked emperor parades by. We know what the child does not. The Emperor believes it is only he who cannot see his beautiful garments. He is duped by conmen pretending to be highly skilled tailors. They sew and weave fabric and thread that do not actually exist while pocketing the large amount of money they claim to have spent on the extravagant fabric. The courtiers around the Emperor also don't say anything. Either they believe it is only they who cannot see the royal garments or they believe if they say something that contradicts the Emperor, they will surely suffer.

The child on the street certainly is not the only one to notice that the Emperor was naked. There may have been a few whose denial was so profound that they saw beautiful garments where there were none. But naked is naked, and naked while parading down the street is hard to miss.

However, the child is the only one to say what must have been obvious to everyone: the Emperor is not wearing any clothes! Once the child proclaims the obvious, everyone else freely admits to what was going on. The Emperor is exposed and devoid of all garments and ornaments of royal superiority.

He had previously been unaware of his situation, or at least unwilling to admit it. A victim of his own denial and squandered precious resources on illusion, he was stripped of the vestments of power, wisdom, authority, and strength... by a child! Having had the naked truth about him revealed, the community ridicules him, but keeping his head held high, he strides back into his lonely castle, naked and stunned in silent shame.

Like "The Emperor's New Clothes," *The Gospel of Loneliness* dispels harmful myths, stories, stereotypes, stigmas, and archaic traditions that we internalize that tell us that we should not believe our own eyes, trust our own instincts, or confront customs and authorities that purport to know best how we should behave, think, feel, worship, and love.

"The Emperor's New Clothes" shows people who doubted themselves because of the consensus of public opinion and observation. But not the child. We learn from a child that we can be faithful to our beliefs, even if those around us claim that we are wrong. In the Bible, the person we call Doubting Thomas was willing to proclaim doubt among the crowd of unanimous believers. That can be a lonely situation.

Was the Emperor lonely in his nakedness? Was the child lonely in being the only one to proclaim truth in a mob intoxicated by falsehood? We can learn about loneliness from "The Emperor's New Clothes" and not deny, minimize, rationalize, or denigrate our state of loneliness because of some myth fed to us by a tinker, tailor, soldier, pastor, boss, scribe, systemic flaw, or institution that makes us feel naked, vulnerable, and lonely when we speak up. There is no need to hide our loneliness in parades, fancy clothing, community gatherings, or even worship services thinking that loneliness is some sort of deficit. We need not hope that no one will see our true state for fear that we will be judged or pitied by the community. Loneliness is not something that needs to be covered up. It needs to be exposed and proclaimed.

The Loneliness of Isaac

> "'The fire and wood are here,' Isaac said, 'but where is the lamb for the burnt offering?'" — Genesis 22:7

In addition to the obedience of Abraham, the graciousness of God, and the sacrifice of the ram instead of the human, let's look at this story through the lonely eyes of Isaac.

Nothing about Isaac warranted his death other than being the trusting son of his father. The boychild, Abraham's only son, walked innocent and devout, with his father toward the site of worship and sacrifice. Abraham had Isaac carry the wood upon which he would be killed, just like one day Jesus would carry the wood cross upon which he would be killed.

When they arrived at the site, Isaac asked the whereabouts of the lamb for the sacrifice. Abraham said that God would provide the lamb. Abraham took the wood, built an altar, bound Isaac's hands, laid his son upon the wood, pulled out his knife, and prepared to kill his child.

Just in the nick of time, God intervened through an angel who praised Abraham for his willingness to sacrifice his son on behalf of God. Abraham was instructed to sacrifice a ram instead of his child.

God promised Abraham many offspring and the conquest of his enemies. God promised Isaac nothing. Father and son returned home together.

We never hear from Isaac; not a word, thought or feeling. The least I can do for this child is to give voice to his loneliness and isolation by offering my own words, thoughts, and feelings.

Isaac had survived his father. I believe he was grateful and yet perplexed. He wanted to believe this happened for a reason and was part of God's plan. But I also believe Isaac might never trust his father again, even to go for a walk. Isaac must have wondered if his mother was in on the plot. He was probably curious if his father always followed voices in his head claiming to be God.

Isaac's near death was averted, but he may have wondered what might come next. He must have found it strange that his father never explained what had happened and why. How lonely Isaac must have been with a God, mother, and father who remained silent in the midst of such violence and pain.

This story, framed in terms of obedience to God and willingness to make deep personal sacrifice, makes me feel the loneliness of Isaac in my own life and times. We have become quite good at sacrificing others. We sacrifice children on the pyre of inequity of schools and education. Who gets saved and who gets burned seems so unjust. It is peculiar, for example, that God decided to sacrifice a ram instead of Isaac, but not a ram instead of Jesus. So Isaac was freed from death on a funeral pyre but must have felt... burned. Jesus was left on the cross and, according to his own words, felt forsaken.

I don't want scripture to create loneliness in me as this story does. When we will begin to comfort, console, and nurture rather than ignore the lonely Isaac within us and each other? I want us to feel empowered to preach and to demand preaching on these texts of terror, abandonment, and loneliness, realizing that it is often through bad news that we locate Good News. We must accept that sometimes the Isaacs of the world may not heal in the ways and timeframe that we prefer.

The lonely and those who fall and cannot get back up are as much our siblings as the heroic and triumphant who are heralded as exemplars of obedience and faith. Awareness and compassionate acceptance of loneliness in self and others is a spiritual awakening. Admissions of doubt and alienation are courageous acts that empowers us to get off the funeral pyre and return to our village with or without tacit acceptance of the whims of our father on earth attributed to our Father who art in heaven.

A Lonely Child in Ruby Slippers

At the end of the movie *The Wizard of Oz*, all Dorothy needs to do to return to her family, friends, and home is to click her heels three times. According to the good witch Glinda, Dorothy possessed the power to get back home all along. Then why wasn't she told at the beginning of the movie, rather than at the end? That would have saved her a lot of trouble with flying monkeys, a wicked witch, a conman pulling levers of power, and almost lapsing into a drug-induced stupor while traversing a field of poppies.

Glinda did not tell Dorothy at the beginning that Dorothy always had the power to get back home by clicking her heels because Dorothy wasn't ready to receive the message. She wouldn't have believed it. Dorothy needed the experiences along the Yellow Brick Road to discover that what she thought was missing from her life was available to her all along. She needed to know the loneliness of losing to appreciate what she had.

The Wicked Witch of the West flies on her broom and paints "SURRENDER DOROTHY" in the sky. Scary image, for me, to this day! As a child, I kept it a secret that, if I were Dorothy, I would have surrendered the moment I saw the writing in the sky. Many of us were taught that to surrender means defeat and is the opposite of victory. However, it is only through surrender that you get to live another day. Imagine that Dorothy saw "SURRENDER DOROTHY" in the sky and thought it meant:

- ❀ Surrender the ego that demands a certain outcome.
- ❀ Surrender the "fight or lose" mentality.
- ❀ Surrender the belief that you need to find some powerful man pulling levers to make things happen.
- ❀ Surrender to the inherent loneliness of separation from that which you love and surrender the fear you cannot live without it.
- ❀ Surrender to the fact that we don't always get to choose our spiritual lessons, teachers, and classrooms.
- ❀ Surrender to the possibility that every journey, pilgrimage, and relationship may be part of your spiritual maturation if you adjust your expectations, perceptions, and strategy.

Dorothy got by with a little help from her friends. But it was *her* journey. Being with her friends actually helped her realize how lonely she was. She was lonely even in a technicolor world with her colorful friends and lollipop kids. Her friends were helpful. But skipping down a yellow brick road from one experience to another with interesting friends is not, in and of itself, a solution to loneliness. Dorothy and her friends felt that part of them was missing and they were incomplete. What they had in common was a longing, a loneliness that inspired them to stay on their path. Loneliness was part of their solidarity.

After clicking her heels three times, Dorothy awoke where her journey began, but with a new consciousness! She realized in Oz that life is not a black-and-white dead-end field of dust and wind, but is a technicolor world in which she found a long and winding yellow brick road that led her to the center of her own soul and relationships.

But first she needed to take the first step of the journey upon it. It was only after she became willing to be lonely and willing to take her first step on a new path that she met three acquaintances, each embodying a part of Dorothy's developing sense of self: a heart, a brain, and courage.

I do not relate well to "there's no place like home." My reaction to that is "thank God!" I have no nostalgia or longing for my childhood home. My childhood home was a hellhole and you couldn't drag me back there. I did, however, have a sense of what "home" might be. If I were Dorothy, I would have stayed in Oz. My lack of a secure, affirming, and accepting home was a propellant to somehow someday find a sense of home within myself not contingent on any particular group of people, places, or things. If I could be at home within myself, I figured, then I could be at home everywhere.

I knew I would have to say "welcome home" to loneliness as well as to other things I did not like. Any home has people you are more comfortable with than others. Loneliness was like a family member with whom I did not always feel comfortable. But I never thought to try to evict or disown it. Loneliness was part of me and part of the family.

If I am lonely, I told myself, I have a compass directing me to wholeness. Loneliness was a guide that could lead me first to a home within myself, then a community to call home, then perhaps to a church to call home.

At various times in the past several years, I have left a community I was reluctant to leave, but I was still at home within myself. I left a church home to which I no longer felt called, but I still was at home with God. I left a house I no longer needed but I was still at home as I went elsewhere. I even lost myself, for a while, after the sudden death of my young daughter, but she still has a home in me. All that remained of me, at that juncture in my life, was loneliness, and loneliness was still a connection to love.

Life is, as the saying goes, more about the journey than the destination. Dorothy learned that you do not need to leave to arrive. She never left the farm. It was all a dream. And yet her mind, heart, and soul were changed forever. Life no longer needed to be merely endured.

With new consciousness, even the most mundane aspects of her life could be celebrated and cherished. The longed-for place that she believed only existed somewhere over the rainbow was within her all along. God was within. Family was within. With such insight, experience, and wisdom, her life was transformed.

Like Dorothy, we must discover what is missing before we can appreciate what we have. We must travel our own long and winding yellow brick road where we may encounter loneliness, link arms with it, and continue on down the road. Only then will it be time to click our heels three times, and be restored, reunited, and transformed.

The Loneliness of The Scarlet Letter

> "Injustice and filth they throw after the lonely one . . .
> they hate the lonely one." — Friedrich Nietzsche[8]

Nathaniel Hawthorne's *The Scarlet Letter*, set in colonial Puritan Massachusetts, tells the story of Hester Prynne, whose husband is presumed lost at sea. She has an affair, which results in her bearing a child named Pearl. As punishment for her adultery, Hester is brought to a scaffold where she endures public humiliation by being forced to wear a scarlet-colored letter A on her clothing. The assembled spectators demand to know who the father of the child is, but she refuses to name him.

Hester's stigma, shame, loneliness, and isolation bear similarities between the Scarlet Letter A for adultery and the Scarlet Letter L for loneliness.

Hester and Pearl live a quiet life in a cottage on the edge of town where Hester embroiders for a meager living. In this marginalized existence, Pearl becomes troubled to the point that Hester is threatened with the loss of custody. The child is collateral damage in the shaming of her mother by the community, and by her unnamed father who plays no part in her life. Pearl, like her mother, is lonely, isolated, and has no friends.

The father of the child is Hester's pastor, the Rev. Arthur Dimmesdale. Hester endures *public* shame, stigma, and humiliation. Dimmesdale endures *private* shame and fear of exposure. He becomes ill and his family doctor sees the letter A appear, like a stigmata, on his chest. Dimmesdale recovers.

Time passes. Their respective loneliness seems to be a catalyst for creativity. Hester Prynne's embroidery is magnificent. Dimmesdale's sermons become better and better! She refuses to be confined and defined by the expectations of others. He is better able to extend compassion and empathy to his congregation. They confess their struggles, sins, and loneliness to him, finding relief and forgiveness. He confesses his struggles, sins, and loneliness to no one and begins to rot from the inside out.

One day, Dimmesdale returns to the same scaffold where Hester Prynne bore the wrath alone for what they had done together. He reveals what he has done, confesses his love for Hester, collapses, and dies in Hester's arms.

Hester returns home and continues wearing the scarlet letter. Why return to the scene of so much pain? Had she discovered that the site of loneliness can also be the site of healing? Had the scarlet letter for Adultery lost its meaning, and been replaced by the scarlet letter A for Acceptance?

Upon her death, Hester Prynne was buried near Dimmesdale. They share one tombstone, upon which is chiseled the letter A. Did their love endure despite the loneliness, isolation, and shame, or because of it?

Hester Prynne's husband was lost at sea and she was lonely. Dimmesdale was the leader of a congregation and secretly lonely. By not naming him, she endured stigma and shame but revealed integrity and conviction. By not naming himself, Arthur enabled her stigma and shame and revealed his *lack* of integrity and conviction. And yet, the letter A appeared on his fevered chest, apparently in solidarity with her.

Lonely people bear a scarlet letter L, invisible to the naked eye but still there. People can sense it, and they avoid the lonely bearer of it.

In many respects, not much has changed. Alice, a recently widowed woman, came to talk with me. She told me that she was no longer invited to dinner parties at the homes of church members. Her friends had become uncomfortable around her. Lonely widows can be seen by friends as threatening because they that might attract their husbands.

Alice and the former friends were living in a gated community built to protect them from intruders. That community had now locked and gated their doors and hearts against the perceived threat posed by their friend who had become a lonely widow.

The stigma of the affair between Hester and Dimmesdale kept them from admitting it and it resulted in loneliness. Perhaps the congregation failed to recognize and address this loneliness because of their own stigma and denial. How would you feel if your pastor stood in the pulpit and proclaimed their deep loneliness and how it was affecting their ministry? Would fear of your reaction keep your pastor from being honest with the congregation? Would you think that a clergyperson should have issues of loneliness resolved if they were spiritually fit? Would you see their loneliness as some sort of weakness or social maladaptation?

It is through their wounds that Hester and Arthur were healed. It would be a source of healing for clergy, laity, and gated-neighborhood residents alike to be as free to confess their loneliness as they are to confess their love. A spiritual life is often a lonely life. All these people could have been lovingly lonely together instead of stigmatized and lonely apart.

A Crucified Lonely Christ

How lonely Jesus may have been as he walked the Stations of the Cross through the streets of Jerusalem. Was there really nothing that anyone could do to help? There are no mentions of throngs of soldiers surrounding Jesus as he carried his cross through the streets. He never told people not to try to rescue him. But there were plenty of people denying they even knew him.

Midrash says his followers were told by Jesus that these events were preordained and they were to witness the unfolding horror and live to tell it to the likes of us. Even if Jesus had accepted this as his fate, would that make it any less lonely for him? Or is this our way of reconciling ourselves to the loneliness of our powerlessness as our loved one dies?

How lonely it may have been for Jesus as he gazed down from the cross and saw horrified spectators and sad and silent friends, family, and followers at the foot of his cross.

It must have been lonely to see women weeping, men paralyzed, and children horrified by the sight of his eyes leaking life. How lonely it might have been for someone to feel that they could have done something to get Jesus down from the cross but didn't.

It is said that no Christian ever dies alone because God is always there. But loneliness drips from Jesus's last words while he was dying on the cross, "God, why have you forsaken me?" How lonely I feel right now as I ponder Jesus dying with an overwhelming sense of forsakenness.

Even the word loneliness is so threatening and maligned that our spiritual leaders strive to be above, beyond, or immune to it. I have never heard anyone talk about why the people at the foot of the cross did not rise up to bring him down. I have never heard anyone in church, seminary, home, or in a book speak about Jesus being lonely. In so doing is it us that have forsaken Jesus? I remain uncertain that God did not want us to intervene.

I am sorry, precious Jesus, that you died with thorns of loneliness cutting into your head. The loneliness in you is part of the Christ I feel in me.

6

Lonely in the Pulpit and the Pew

Lonely in the Pulpit

Many of us are aware of the connection between loneliness and illness. Fewer of us make the connection between loneliness and blessedness. Praying for a cure is easier than taking action for prevention. Perhaps we are reluctant to admit our powerlessness to control outcomes.

It is understandable to avoid what we fear. We proclaim victory over loneliness as we emerge from a pandemic but retreat from it when we say little about our personal and congregational loneliness as our churches shrink and people disappear. Admitting fear for the future of the church to a congregation that needs our strength may render us vulnerable. So we proclaim God will do for us that which we cannot do for ourselves. And then we do too much by ourselves for fear that God is not doing for us quickly enough. We burn the midnight oil until we burnout, writing sermons that fewer and fewer come to hear.

Countless times we hear pastors proclaim, "I am angry!" but rarely, if ever, do we hear them say, "I am lonely." The time has come to say it out loud. Loneliness is only loneliness. No more. No less.

The Loneliness of Prophetic Witness

If you want to talk yourself into remaining silent about your prophetic witness to the church you serve, read the prophets of Hebrew scripture. Speaking truth to power in even the faintest way to those not inclined to like or listen to it is not always good for professional longevity.

A pastor who is prophetic in her calling often feels compelled to confront the most troubling parts of the church, community, and world. However, a congregation can lament the way it is and long for the way it was. Some of those finally freed from the pharaoh in the Book of Exodus almost immediately began to long for the "good old days" when they at least had a meal and a place to sleep. A prophet is a window to the world and a mirror to the congregation, helping it to see itself as it is, despite its reluctance to do so.

The loneliness of prophetic witness and the unfavorable reception it might engender can be a big issue for pastors. You always alienate yourself, in at least a little way, every time you speak truth to power; especially if you are not backed by your congregation or community. And that can be a very lonely experience. There is a big difference between a church that's got your back and a church that might stab you in the back when you bring a social justice agenda into the sanctuary.

In the church that I serve as pastor, during a Sunday morning service, a homeless man received a shampoo and a haircut on the chancel. The pulpit had been removed to make room for a portable shampoo sink and barber chair. A Jewish musician raised in apartheid South Africa sang "Lean on Me." The Confirmation Class youth read excerpts from Matthew 25. No verbal sermon was necessary.

The message was preached by getting the ministries out of the back of the church and revealing their witness from the center of the chancel.

I did not know how to pull it off or how it would go over. I was torn between boldness and insecurity because I didn't want people to be upset. But it was a risk I was willing to take in response to what God wanted me to do.

At times like this, I am lonely and insecure in my ministry. I am not a hero in this story. I feel compelled to both follow my call and to cash my paycheck. Following my call is far lonelier than I ever thought when I attended Union Theological Seminary. I wish they had offered a course on loneliness, or at least included it in the courses that included everything but.

A pastor friend invited a migrant worker activist to speak at her church. The pastor was relatively new to her position and was quite surprised when, the next day, she was criticized by the irate congregation that did not want to hear about immigration from the pulpit or elsewhere.

At first, she felt lonely and isolated from the loving congregation that she thought she knew. Loneliness and isolation were joined by fear and insecurity when she received a threat from key church leaders. If she continued to bring social justice into the church, she would be fired. That response created more loneliness when the pastor and congregation realized how much separation had occurred in the time between Sunday sermon and Monday morning reaction. They tried to gloss it over and let bygones be bygones. It didn't work.

Back in the parsonage, she read the prophets in the Old Testament. She felt in her loneliness that she was in good company.

But it was still loneliness. She was fortunate, in a way, that her congregation was immediately vocal in their reaction. At least she was able to clearly see one of the subtle ways in which pastors are shushed into silence by a congregation content with intentional deafness and blindness to what was going on outside the beautiful stained glass of the church.

People enter seminary for many reasons. I came to ordained ministry seeking a new family to compensate for the family I never had as a child.

I got a family, alright! In my church family there was the equivalent of a drunken uncle who always arrives late and belligerent for Thanksgiving dinner. There was also the kind and selfless grandma who just wants me to be happy. I also received competitive siblings, an older sister who dotes on me, and a cousin who resents me. Then came relatives who unexpectedly supported me. I got Judas. I got Jesus. I didn't get what I expected, and I got more than I hoped for. Blessings and curses often come in the same gift-wrapped box. I received love. And I received loneliness.

Clergy families are often lonely. First there is having to move to a new location and congregation, which is exciting but also unfamiliar. There is the potential loneliness of making new connections and friendships and comparing them disappointedly to previous ones in the prior place of residence. As sometimes happens, there is a blowup. The clergy family moves on and are subjected to loneliness again.

A pastor told me that all it would take to make a difference in the loneliness of her and her family is one empathic person to acknowledge how difficult their transition to a new community and church had been. And yet, somehow, so many churches haven't figured that out. "I am fully aware," she said, "that I was called to serve them and not the other way around. I know that Jesus washed people's feet, but he also accepted their offer to wash his."

Clergy are often perceived more for the role they perform, than as the person they are. I was in an elevator when I saw a person I somewhat knew. We chatted and when the elevator reached her floor she said, "Have a nice day, pastor."

The doors closed. A woman and I were then the sole occupants of the elevator. She turned to me and said, "I had an abortion in college and I have never forgiven myself." Her eyes filled with tears. The elevator doors opened. She stepped out, turned back, and gave me a waist-high wave goodbye. The doors closed again and I continued in the elevator until I reached the floor of my dentist. I thought about the pain she must have been in to have blurted out that elevator confession to me.

That encounter was twenty years ago and I have not forgotten. I still wonder if I should have walked out of the elevator with her to continue the conversation. Or was her confession to me, a stranger and a pastor, all she needed or wanted? She was clearly lonely and burdened.

Part of my loneliness is that she chose to confide in me because she heard a woman in the elevator call me "pastor." In a way, I feel grateful. But sometimes when someone confides in me because I am a pastor, it seems so non-reciprocal. She somewhat trusted me. Sometimes people just need to vent. I get it. But sometimes, as clergy, I feel like a vending machine. I know a bit about family systems theory and transference. But sometimes, I wonder if I am seen as merely a functionary. That makes me feel lonely.

A non-reciprocal relationship between clergy and parishioner is disempowering. It is lonely to have a role in a relationship that may appear mutual but is not. Relationships are reciprocal or they are not relationships.

Clergy loneliness is often triggered by holidays when other families with children are off duty, but the church family is on double duty. Our Sunday school director and I live next door to each other. After a church meeting one night in December, we both pulled into our respective driveways at the same time. The Sunday school director noted that our two houses were the only ones on the block that were not decorated. We were busy bringing Christmas to congregations, but not as much to our own homes. Part of the pain was knowing exactly how busy each of us were, having awareness that it did not seem quite right, and also knowing there was little we could do about it.

There are occasions in scripture when people are lured or forced into the wilderness, the go-to place for mystics, prophets, poets, pastors, priests, and seekers. Jesus went into the wilderness for forty days and when he emerged his ministry began. Saints lived there. Contemplatives found quality silence there. John the Baptizer did his thing there. Visionaries get the best reception for their antennas there.

Unfortunately, many in the pulpit and the pew are afraid to go there. Jesus the carpenter and the table-turner is one thing; but the mystical Jesus of the transfiguration is another. God beckons us into the desert on the outskirts of town, the wilderness within, the thin place, and the night of the soul. I have been to the wilderness of land and of soul many times. Each time I fear I might not find a way out. And yet I go there. Some things are faced best when faced alone.

Loneliness is a component of spiritual transformation. It's an expression of faith. We can choose to believe and accept faith. Faith brings us closer to our God of many names such as creator, Higher Power, and Mother Nature. Faith brings us closer to others through the realization we are all connected.

Two fine people are members of the church I serve, though they are infrequent attendees. When their elderly parent was dying, I periodically checked in with them, offering to visit with the parent. I was politely told they would let me know.

One night I received a text saying the mother passed away and that they were having the service at a neighboring church in accordance with the parent's wish. The pastor of that church is a close friend and confidant, and our churches are in the same denomination. I texted back to the couple, expressing condolences and an offer of support.

The next day I called the pastor to ask if I may be of assistance. During the conversation, I learned that the members of my church had been coming to his church fairly regularly for the past few months. He also told me that he had been visiting the recently deceased parent for quite a while.

I told him that both children of the deceased are members of my church. He knew that and I was surprised he did not tell me about this. He responded that he never asks people about their lives or membership elsewhere. I told him that when members of my church are attending his church, and when he began making pastoral visits to the dying parent, he should have told me. I told him that a friend and colleague making pastoral visits to the home of one of our church members is inappropriate.

I felt lonely and conflicted. I could not turn to colleagues in our denomination because they would know who I was talking about. It seemed there was nowhere to turn for confidential, safe communication. I wondered if this kind of loneliness and isolation winnows the field of prospective pastors. Being numb was not an option. But I felt raw. Parish ministry seems to alternate between being frustrating, boring, frightening, and lonely.

I did not burden the members of my church who are the children of the deceased with this. I went to the wake at the funeral home, but not the church service at which my friend presided. This situation led me to some questions:

- ❀ Where do pastors turn with such issues? Do they talk to colleagues in the same denomination?

- ❀ Do they talk to their partners and spouses? What if they have no such person? And even if they did, who can understand ministry situations if they are not involved in ministry?

- ❀ Is it right to contact clergy associations outside of their denomination or faith tradition?

❀ Who is it safe to trust with confidential information and situations?

❀ How do pastors handle disappointment and loneliness generated by congregation members?

❀ What do you do if praying, thinking, and writing are not helping?

❀ Is loneliness a spiritual gift if it has brought you these questions?

❀ Can a pastor who is open about loneliness be a spiritual gift to their congregation?

❀ Does loneliness make a pastor more compassionate, passionate, and merciful?

Lonely in the Pew

A man sits alone inside an empty church, the amber light of dusk seeps through large stained-glass windows as shadows of the ends of pews stretch like prison bars across the floor of the aisle. An empty cross in an empty sanctuary looms large on a wall in the distance. Is he alone? Is he lonely? Is it true that you can never truly be alone because God is always present?

An elderly woman, alone in a cemetery, leans on her walker, looking down at a headstone as misty rain washed it clean. The flowers, still wrapped in green tissue with a red ribbon tied tight near the stems, lie on the moist ground next to the empty vase at the foot of the marker. Is her loneliness a problem to be solved or a blessing to be received?

Night does not mean the sun has gone away, but is merely hidden from view waiting to be "born again" when conditions are right. The same is true with loneliness.

I attended a Zoom meeting about new research on the pandemic and its effects on congregations. Towards the end of the program, we were instructed to write our questions in the Q&A

tab at the bottom of the screen. Some of the questions were selected by the moderator who then read them to the panel.

I wrote in the Q&A box: "Did your research reflect an increase of loneliness during the pandemic and did that affect congregations?" The moderator chose my question and posed it to the panel. However, he substituted the word isolation for loneliness.

You may perhaps think that he thought loneliness and isolation are synonymous. They are not. Even if he did think they are synonymous, why didn't he use the word as written in the question? He just couldn't bring himself to use the word loneliness. There is the Scarlet Letter L once again. He rewrote my question into one that I had not asked.

It annoyed me. People already have done enough erasing and redefining of loneliness.

The Elephant in the Sanctuary

Loneliness is the elephant in the sanctuary. Whenever something significant is denied, so too is the person who noticed it or brought it up.

When I was a kid, I was shown a drawing of three chimpanzees. One had their hands over their ears, the second had their hands over their eyes, and the third had their hands over their mouth. The caption was "Hear No Evil, See No Evil, Speak No Evil." The deafness, blindness, and muteness did not succeed in making "evil" go away. The drawing did succeed in encouraging children, teachers, and caregivers to close their eyes, ears, and mouth to innumerable offenses.

Change the word evil to loneliness and see what happens. "Hear No Loneliness, See No Loneliness, Speak No Loneliness" does not succeed in making loneliness go away. It does succeed in encouraging children and adults to close themselves off from others. As if they had done something wrong or worse yet, as if there was something wrong with them.

This idea is embodied in the telephone calls made to a clergyperson asking about things that either do not need to be immediately answered or could more easily be answered by someone else. Rarely will someone speak frankly or directly about loneliness. So loneliness is tacitly kept by pastor and parishioner. Such calls are a good sign of being willing to reach out. But they often address only a symptom of loneliness, not the source. People may also be depressed, or feel their loneliness is a hopeless situation, and do not even make a phone call.

What is called for *is not* the "outing" of someone who is suspected of being in a closet of loneliness from which they fear to emerge. What *is* called for is recognizing the lonely ones in our midst as persons gifted with the predisposition of compassion for others.

The Loneliness of Not Being Welcomed

In many congregations, guests told me they have experienced the loneliness of not being heartily welcomed in churches, parties, and other community events. This is particularly ironic because every church I have ever visited or read about has proclaimed that they are friendly and welcoming. Some have proclaimed they are "extravagantly hospitable!"

Often, though not always, hospitality and welcoming have strings attached. Some people have been called, even before they got home from their first visit to church, and were asked to attend a committee, board, or fellowship meeting. They feel the "really nice" people at church were looking for warm bodies and fat wallets to help the church survive. A few even reported feeling "pounced on." And the ones that get pounced on first are often the ones who most closely resemble the dominant ethnicity and culture of the congregation.

I assume these situations are exceptions to, and not representative of, most churches. People come to churches and support groups for a variety of reasons, including loneliness. Let us be careful not to magnify their loneliness by immediately assessing them on their potential ability to be useful to us. We are called not to be served but to serve.

The Loneliness of Disappointment

A volunteer comes to the church soup kitchen and when they arrive are kindly told to come back the next time because they have all the help they need that day. No one is trying to hurt the feelings of the volunteer. They simply don't need them. The volunteer goes home and never returns to try to volunteer again.

Think about how the person felt on their pilgrimage to the volunteer site. They may have believed they would be doing something beneficial for the community that would make a difference. Perhaps they were excited about meeting new and interesting people. They may have looked forward to calling loved ones or posting on social media about trying to do some good in this hurting world and inspiring others to do likewise. None of that happened.

These thwarted hopes were, most likely, stuffed deep within themselves. They may criticize themselves for having an ulterior motive of volunteering just to feel good about themselves rather than for selfless service. The result is they may lapse into feeling disappointment over a wish that was not meant to be. They withdraw even further, turning away from themselves after having been turned away by others. Having experienced this, who would not feel lonely?

Disappointment makes us feel separated from, not connected to others. Few can withstand this for long. Like the slow drip of minerals that form a stalactite in a cave, disappointments may eventually cause people to become hard, immovable, and lonely.

The Loneliness of Not Fitting Into Church

I know that pompous people are loose in our midst. But most people I know think far less of themselves than we think of them, and certainly less of themselves than God thinks of them. Some people I know are struggling to climb up to low self-esteem. Imagine then walking into a church for the first time wondering if they will fit in.

Other people feel they don't fit into church because they've changed. Recently, a couple in our church separated. The mother and daughter moved away. The father feels lonely and disoriented in church without them. Church no longer fits. I contacted him, but I doubt he will return. No hard feelings.

Loneliness for Yesterday

Some people are lonely for the former church, the way their church once was and the people they once knew.

A church member recently told me, "I see what you are trying to do here," she said. "But the music is not for me. Younger people like it. I am glad the church is bringing in new people but I don't know anyone here anymore. There is good attendance here today, Dwight, but I barely know any of them. The section where I sit is emptying out. My friends are dying or moving. The area near the piano where the young people like to sit is filling up. I get it. But coming to church makes me lonely."

I am also lonely for the people that she is lonely for. Many knew each other for decades. They are collectively and individually lonely for their own and each other's children. Memories of pageants abound. Dusty, ragged robes of the Three Wise Ones hang in a basement closet. Teacups and saucers in kitchen cabinets have been waiting for tea to be poured into them for years.

And COVID-19 has not been merciful or kind. Our church is 230 years old and has never been closed for nearly as long as it was closed by COVID-19. An assisted living facility a few doors down opened a few years ago. It is full. Our church is not.

The dignified elderly woman who told me that she was lonely for the way church used to be was clearly saying goodbye without, it seems, even knowing it. And without saying it or even knowing it, I was saying goodbye to her as well.

Anyone who is not lonely is not aware and awake. Some say that the touchstone of change is pain. But I believe the touchstone of change is loneliness. It is our primal, resident state of being. Touching primal loneliness is what allows the sword to be pulled out of the rock. Touching primal loneliness is what allows straw to be spun into gold and silence to be spun into music.

Being lonely for yesterday saves us from bitterness and regret. Loneliness opens hearts that have tried to live unopened. The dignified elderly woman spoke of loneliness for yesterday, but experiencing it today. That is not something to be taken away from her.

The church doesn't need a hospice chaplain; it needs a midwife. We need to bear down and prepare to give birth to the lament that has been gestating in the body of the church for years. Then take a stethoscope and listen to the heartbeat of loneliness. We need to provide and prepare for the as of yet unborn church of tomorrow being birthed from the church of yesterday.

7

The Future of Loneliness

What will loneliness look like in the future? Will it get better, worse, or merely different?

This may not, at first, seem to have much to do with communities such as church. But if people are changing, then relationships are changing. And if relationships are changing, so are communities and churches.

Even our concepts of humanity are changing. The United Nations Declaration of Universal Human Rights may have to change, as our understanding of what rights mean changes, and as our understanding of humans and artificial intelligence changes as well. The wording of welcoming church members may need to be adapted to include robotic persons.

Technological visionaries and engineers are, at this moment, integrating technological means to satiate people's deep needs. If churches believe that spirituality is also a deep need of people and we want to be part of the conversation, we need a willingness and, perhaps, even an eagerness to humbly assess who we now are, and who we are becoming.

Artificial Human Companions

In the Philippines during the COVID-19 epidemic, robots wearing caps and gowns with photos of the faces of human graduating students attached to them, ventured across the stage and each received a diploma. The human students, who attended the graduation ceremony by Zoom, seemed pleased that a creative and fun way to adapt to reality had been made possible by a feat of engineering. Not long after, there were robotic bartenders and housekeepers at the 2022 Winter Olympics in Beijing, China.

Now imagine a robot pastor offering prayers in your church for a human congregation. Then picture a robot pastor entering a contamination room at a hospital to visit a dying victim of a global pandemic caused by a virus for which there is no vaccine or cure. What about robots serving as deacons and collecting the offering? Imagine robots changing diapers in the church nursery. Does this sound like fantasy or prophecy?

Funerals for Robot Pets

In 2018, a traditional Japanese funeral was held in a 450-year-old Buddhist temple for robot dogs. The priest dismissed the idea that memorials for machines is silly or wrong, saying that all things have a bit of soul. The robot dogs were the beloved companions to the many owners who attended the funeral service. The humans grieving robotic dogs were indistinguishable from people grieving the loss of a real dog. In the future, even stronger bonds of love between humans and machines will be forged in the quest for an end to loneliness, especially as technology improves.

Imagine a robot dog going tirelessly from room to room in a nursing home, hospital, or hospice center to comfort patients. You actually do not need to imagine it because robotic comfort dogs were introduced in early 2023. Robopets may even be effective in helping people experiencing memory loss. Robot dogs could guard the church and bark at intruders. Imagine playing with a robot dog as a reward for doing well on a Sunday school test. Just imagine.

Robot Chess Champion, Astronaut, Psychotherapist

If someone can have a meaningful relationship with a robot dog, and even provide it an expensive funeral, it does not take much to envision a day when someone can have a meaningful relationship with a robotic human, and provide a funeral as well.

If an artificial human companion and a flesh-and-blood human reside together and are particularly close, they may choose to go to church together. They may decide to be buried together as well.

Humans have been buried with instruments and machines. Jazz musician Miles Davis was reportedly buried with one of his trumpets. Wild Bill Hickok was buried with his rifle. Lonnie Holloway was buried in his 1973 Pontiac. Many people are buried with their artificial knees, hips, heart valves, and teeth. Why not be buried with your robot?

We are also already living and having relationships with inanimate objects. We ask Siri for directions. The disembodied voice named Alexa tells us jokes and we laugh at them. Children sleep with stuffed animals that aren't living beings to us, but they certainly seem to be living beings to children.

Relationships with objects are nothing new. But they are becoming more frequent and sophisticated. We can now literally talk to our refrigerator and the refrigerator responds. We can tell our house to turn off the lights, lock or unlock the door, and lower the room temperature. Even before such inventions, many people thought of their house as a living being. Didn't they used to make horror movies about this?

In August 2019, Russia announced they are sending the first robot astronaut into space. The robot's first duties will be routine maintenance of the craft with the goal of the robot eventually performing space walks.

It is not difficult to imagine that robotic humans with programmable relationships may replace or become alternatives to human relationships that are so often fraught with difficulties. Artificial humans are already being tested as psychotherapists. Perhaps artificial human relationships will have an impact on the divorce rate in America. There is no need to divorce a robotic human companion. They can be programmed to change attitudes and mannerisms as their owner changes in age, attitudes, abilities, and preferences.

Artificial humans may be programmed to be better chaplains in hospitals that human ones. A robot, could receive daily updates on chaplaincy. Artificial humans might conduct last rites or spoken prayers on demand at any hour. They can be on call 24/7 and reside at the hospital. A human chaplain at home in pajamas could ask ChatGPT to write a prayer for a patient with a particular condition. The robotic chaplain could go to the bedside of the patient at the hospital and pray the prayer the human chaplain wrote from home.

Robots could staff hotlines for utility companies and be programmed to recognize our fear as we report a lack of light during a power outage. Just imagine a robot leading us to the light, and restoring our sense of a loss of power and autonomy, and addressing it on emotional, intellectual, and physical levels. We teach computers to sort and route calls to doctors, social service agencies, airlines, and other companies. Nonhumans could be first responders.

Nonhuman companions may even teach how to care for a human. An intermittently inconsolable, screaming, mechanical baby that wets its diaper in the middle of the night will be a pregnancy deterrent to teens. The teens who took a non-human infant home had lower birth rates before the age of twenty than those who did not take a non-human infant home.[9]

Artificial human adult companions can help people in a time when loneliness is increasingly a major factor of life all around the world.

Robot Chaplains, Robot Clergy, Robot Friends

Relationships with artificial chaplains are not only possible, some claim they are preferable. The body parts of artificial chaplains may last longer than human chaplains and can be traded in for updated versions. We already wear artificial leather jackets that feel and look real. In the not-so-distant future, the skin and body temperature of nonhuman chaplains may also look and feel increasingly real.

If Alexa already can deliver a joke on demand, an artificial clergyperson should soon be able to be programmed to recognize the parishioner's sense of humor. Software could detect when, how often, and at what subjects you most frequently laugh, and the robot pastor can adapt accordingly. Even the delivery of the words could be provided in the tone, tenor, and pace that you prefer. A robot pastor could change its sense of humor to adapt to your sense of humor. The humor, attitude, demeanor and tone could change with each person who enters the pastor's office. A robotic clergyperson, unlike a merely human one, is always available, pleasant, awake, aware, humorous, and very pastoral.

As computer capabilities rapidly advance, an artificial human friend at your home could detect vocal inflections indicating anger, sadness, joy, and loneliness. It could respond effectively to soothe feelings and help adjust thoughts and attitudes. Your robot friend might suggest you stream certain songs that you most often turn to in times of turmoil.

If you are getting a little emotionally off-balance and are unaware of it, your artificial human companion will understand and respond quickly and appropriately. When your body temperature rises, your nonhuman friend or roommate might ask if you took your medications. Robots could express compassionate concern, exhibit undistracted attention, and suggest you call your doctor or do it for you.

Artificial Human Sex Partner

Let's suppose your artificial human companion welcomes you home after a long day of frustrating and annoying human interactions at work. Your companion, who is never exhausted, makes a suggestion that you engage in your favorite sex act with it, that it already recognizes because it is programmed to detect the frequency and intensity of your physical contact with it. Your robot companion is constantly updating data about you. If a new and improved artificial human comes along, you can trade yours in for a new model. No divorce. No alimony. No flack. No problem! Relax. Your artificial human companion is programmed for no hard feelings!

Let's think about you and other real people for a moment. If you could order a flesh-and-blood, real human lover or companion, what characteristics, body features, attitudes, abilities, and beliefs would you include? Even if your answer is "My ideal companion is my present partner" I still want you to write below what it is about your present partner that causes you to say that.

Whether artificial human companions will ever become satisfactory substitutes for humans on a mass scale has yet to be determined. Moving as quickly as technology does, we may not have to wait long to find out. Manufacturers believe they could be beneficial for geographically isolated people, sexual trauma victims using them for a therapeutic reintroduction to sexual activity, and an end to loneliness.

What's Not to Like?

Imagine customers ordering exact replicas of their dead spouses. Manufacturers are already working on this. If technology has created an opportunity for a perfect breed of pet or robotic dog companion to be manufactured on demand, it is naive to think that such an opportunity will never be created with artificial humans.

Many of us, including myself, are already part artificial and part robotic. People have crowns on their teeth, tattoo eyebrows, robotic arms, prosthetic legs, pacemakers, mechanical heart valves, lifted faces, enlarged breasts, butt implants, knee and hip replacements, and a menu of transplanted organs. Even more will be available in the future.

The human companion that people seek, often seems to be a reflection of themselves. Change and progress often occur, however, when one person is polished and shaped by another. But if the option of one human refining another is not available, then despite technological advances, artificial human companions could be of little sociological, psychological, and spiritual use. People could program their artificial humans to reflect their own prejudice and discrimination. They could command their artificial human companion to obediently make coffee, bring their slippers, provide sex on demand, politely argue but never win on issues of politics, religion, race, class, and money.

Without challenges to our beliefs and actions, we could cease to evolve emotionally, intellectually, and spiritually. We will only tolerate and accept relationships that reflect them in the way they want to be seen.

This could produce a gated community of the mind, in which nothing challenging gets in, and nothing challenging gets out. That is clearly what some people want. But such future technological advances devoid of ethics, morals, and spirituality would contribute to a breakdown of community and more loneliness.

What will happen when someone goes to court to proclaim their right to legally marry the robot companion of their choice? Think of "mail order brides" during the Gold Rush when prospectors chose a mate from a catalogue. Think of arranged marriages that still happen in many places of the world. Then think of robots.

The Future of Artificial and Flesh-and-Blood Companions

Could you determine whether a poem was written by a computer or a human being? Many people get the answer wrong when asked to decide whether a poem was written by artificial or human intelligence, people make their decision based on detecting human experience, emotion, ability to love, empathy, creativity, and spirituality.

My first published book was a book of poems. I have over a half of a century of experience with writing poetry. I was asked to read poems and decide whether they were of artificial or human origin. One time I thought the imagery was too random to have been written by a human. Another time, I found empathy, sensitivity, spirituality and purpose in the poem so I thought it could only have been created by a human. Both times I was wrong.

Clearly, my understanding of being human is about empathy, sensitivity, spirituality, purpose, and meaning. An artificial human companion could simulate those attributes. My young adult son had an accident at a health club and was admitted to a hospital. During a visit, we asked an app (ChatGPT) to write a poem about a father visiting his young adult son in a hospital. While not a great poem, it certainly was good enough to have been written by a human like me.

The Book of Genesis indicates God created humankind out of dirt and in God's image. Today, we who were made in God's image are creating artificial beings in our image. Artificial humans could be part of God's continuous evolution of what it means to be human.

There is little doubt whether robotic beings with artificial intelligence will be an increasing part of our lives. They will be. The question is with what qualities and with attributes they will be created and designed.

Artificial human companions will become more widespread due to technological advances and increasing demands from humans who are increasingly lonely, isolated, and unable or unwilling to endure the nuances of human interaction.

The Downward Trend of Communication Skills

"Loneliness does not come from having no people about one, but from being unable to communicate the things that seems important to oneself."
— Carl G. Jung[10]

In the list below, list three things that you wish a person or group of people knew about you that they currently do not. It doesn't have to be from the depths of your soul. Just write any three things:

1.

2.

3.

Now write one reason that corresponds to each of the three things listed above that explains why you are unable or unwilling to reveal them. In other words, what is stopping you?

1.

2.

3.

Do you presently believe you have the communication skills you need to name the things you want people to know about you? Why are you reluctant or unable to communicate these three things about yourself? It is hard to imagine effective communication between people if one person is unwilling to risk disclosure of what they need and desire from the other.

We seem to be experiencing an increasing reluctance or inability to have meaningful and civil discourse. Many people have abandoned their effort to even try because they believe that meaningful, effective communication is basically impossible. If this continues, we may become increasingly lonely. Without an ability and willingness to communicate with others, our ability to maintain relationships will be impaired.

Ever heard of listening? Listening is what sometimes happens when you are not talking. Listening is also when you stop talking *at* someone instead of being *with* someone. The Art of Listening is different from The Art of Pretending to Be Listening that teaches you an eloquent rebuttal while the other person is still talking.

The Art of Listening includes looking the person in the eye while they are speaking to you. People who do not or will not listen tend to be lonely, even if they are in the company of other people who also do not listen. There is nothing more silent and emptier than a room full of people talking but not listening.

Human relationships changed drastically over the last ten to twenty years. We are now so glued to our phones and social media that we're forgetting how to connect with the people in the same room. Artificial human companions may provide communication that some of us still seek, but no longer know how to find.

Loneliness, Smart Phones, and the Internet

When cellphones came along, I thought they were an awesome invention. But I never foresaw a time when people rarely look up anymore. We are becoming a society where electronic connectivity between people replaces face-to-face encounters. We mistake (or prefer) electronic connection to personal connection. Part of the popularity of texting and emailing is avoiding verbal conversation.

There are clearly many benefits to cellphones and other forms of electronic communication. And yet there is much research showing that cellphones and other electronic devices and media are contributing to loneliness.[11] Social media can also create the feeling that everyone other than you are having a great time. People often offer idealized versions of themselves. That can create a sense of loneliness and isolation in those who read these posts.

Let's lighten-up a bit and play a game. Write 1 to 3 words below that would describe your reaction to losing your cellphone:

1.

2.

3.

Some of the responses I received include anxious, frantic, frustrated, isolated, and lonely. Cellphones and other electronic devices connect us to many things including banking, games, and scheduling. But they also connect us to many of the feelings I just listed. Social media and devices are not a cure for loneliness. Not only that, but they may decrease healthy, intimate relationships with friends, lovers, family, and community.

Online Church

Some people join a virtual church where they hope to make deep and meaningful connections to others, to themselves, and to God. Virtual church can be very helpful because it serves people who, for reasons of physical mobility or geographic location, cannot attend a brick and mortar church. Other people might not feel comfortable or welcome in churches in their area. Some churches are not welcoming of LGBTQ+ people, single parents, people of color, people on the autism spectrum, and other life situations. Virtual churches can be tailored to their personal preferences.

First UCC Second Life is such a virtual church where members create an avatar to look and speak like the you that you want to present to the world. You can adjust the lighting or add candles in the sanctuary without needing to get permission. You choose the architecture and décor. The scripture citations, sermon title, theme, and liturgy are provided by the United Church of Christ (UCC) ordained minister.

Some people see unintended negative consequences of virtual churches. On the surface it may seem great that you can populate the church with the people you want to be there. You want all gay? Have it your way. You like all white? That's your right.

But creating avatars may result in inauthentic relationships with virtual people. Virtual church may be absorbed by self-gratification. Comedian John Crist made a parody of a virtual church experience in which you can create a space in which a church "can be even more about me."

The Internet was supposed to lead us to become one big family. But that has fallen short of expectations. We seem to be retreating further into ourselves.

In an age when church attendance is declining, perhaps the assumption that we deeply and unconsciously crave community needs to be reconsidered. While there is evidence that we want connection, it is not necessarily connection to community provided by houses of faith.

Our desire is for connection to ourselves and to extensions of ourselves that we manifest in virtual relationships, including virtual communities that contain virtual churches with avatars as members. We seek an opportunity to exchange monologues. So we search for people who will affirm what we already know about ourselves and our world. And that is the seeds and soil of profound personal and collective loneliness.

In the future we may increasingly construct situations where access is granted only to authorized persons with permission to enter. That means excluding people, thoughts, emotions, and beliefs that challenge a sense of personal security. This may accomplish for people what suburbs and gated communities were once designed to do by limiting exposure and denying access to whatever challenges the status quo.

But as the emotional, intellectual, and spiritual needs of people are increasingly serviced, or appear to be serviced, through the Internet, they will still need to reach outside their cocoon. No problem! You will be able to allow vendors and suppliers to enter your world without having access to your emotional, intellectual, and spiritual life. Does your artificial human companion need batteries? Access granted. Someone wants to enter your world to ask whether you have programmed your artificial human companion to be a subservient stereotype of a woman? Access denied.

Electronic devices and the Internet may keep you comfortable. But they will also keep you lonely, and isolated. As a result, loneliness will possibly become so entrenched, pervasive, and normative that we no longer even see ourselves as lonely. How could I possibly be lonely? I have 3,452 Facebook friends.

There is loneliness deep within us that we experience as emptiness. Often we cannot see it or won't admit it. Waiting for it to disappear on its own does not happen. Hoping it will make this loneliness and emptiness disappear, we try connecting with individuals and groups. But and, once again, it does not go away. We turn from people to technology but loneliness is not replaced by technology.

Emails, tweets, and TikTok are not friends. Social media posts about loneliness do not end loneliness. If we remain lonely, we may begin to panic. We create alarming, provocative, funny, cute, or sad posts and track whether our "friends" increase or decrease. But either way we remain lonely. Then it's on to other social media platforms, telling ourselves we are merely "creating and marketing our brand" when, in actuality, our brand is loneliness. We stay busy with outings and meetings or we stay home and read, phone, or binge watch shows.

In the list below, write three things that you do or have done to connect with a person, group, or something else that made you feel even more lonely.

1.

2.

3.

Congratulations. You have now identified some things that contribute to your loneliness. As we shall soon see, the society that contributes to your loneliness may now want to cure you of it.

The Loneliness Pill

Would you take a pill that could cure loneliness? Would you encourage other people to take it?

We are already medicating some of the *symptoms* of loneliness with antidepressants, sleep aids, alcohol, incessant activity, and other remedies. Imagine a cure for loneliness that would rival the cure for polio in its efficacy.

A neuroscientist at the California Institute of Technology seems to be approaching such a treatment.[12] She studied the brains of solitary mice. Apparently, when mice are isolated, they experience an increased production of a brain chemical associated with fear and aggression. The fearful and aggressive behavior is reversed when the mice are injected with the drug Osanetant, which researchers state could potentially be used as "the loneliness drug."

Imagine the implications for humans. Loneliness leads to isolation; isolation may cause fear and aggression; fear and aggression may create problematic behavior such as domestic violence, self-harm, and workplace conflict. Such conflict may lead to court orders, including incarceration, and that reinforces loneliness. That is a vicious circle.

Imagine we give the "loneliness pill" to high school kids who present symptoms of deep loneliness and isolation, and have a documented tendency toward fear and aggression, like the mice in the study. The loneliness pill could reduce the likelihood that their loneliness might explode into violence. Could the loneliness pill help these young men and potential perpetrators of crime before they act?

Osanetant has been suggested for those sentenced to solitary confinement. Interesting! We sentence someone to solitary confinement and then give them a pill to eliminate the loneliness caused by solitary confinement.

How many lonely people in churches, jobs, relationships, or sparsely populated areas feel like they are already living a life sentence of solitary confinement? The loneliness pill might help treat those waiting for bedtime at the end of yet another lonely day. They can take a pill and no more loneliness. And, perhaps, no genuine healing. But if loneliness is considered to be a huge problem among inmates in solitary confinement, we could try to eliminate solitary confinement instead of loneliness.

However, even if we cannot abolish solitary confinement but we can accept loneliness as a great teacher, then not even solitary confinement or the death of a loved one can throw us off our path. Now that is power!

Perhaps the future of loneliness is a repurposed pill so powerful and effective that it can help us cope with loneliness. But what if the loneliness pill does not actually solve isolation and loneliness? What if it takes away the symptoms so we no longer even care that we are isolated and lonely? Our inclination to look outside of ourselves to find solutions to issues inside ourselves is worth examining. People who have exhausted many quick fixes to such things as loneliness may be ready to explore other opportunities.

- ❈ Would you take the Loneliness Pill?
- ❈ Should it be offered or mandated to others? Who?
- ❈ Are we (or you) too reliant on pharmacology to mend emotional and social needs?
- ❈ Would you seek other sources of health and healing? What are they?

Hitting Bottom and Bouncing Back

Part of loneliness is that people must hit bottom before they can bounce back. Hitting bottom is a rough journey. No one takes their first drink and decides to join AA. No one throws themselves on the mercy of the court before the verdict is in. No one feels lonely for the first time and immediately decides to do whatever they must to lessen or eliminate being lonely ever again.

Hitting bottom may sound like bad news. But it is not nearly as bad as the worst news, which is that, sadly, there are many who do not bounce back.

The good news, as we have established throughout this book, is that while loneliness can be your tormentor, it can also be your teacher, inspiration, and friend. Acceptance that loneliness is part of the human condition is key to change.

You are born alone and you will die alone, even if you are in the company of others. No one can take that heroic journey for you. Death may be stressful, perhaps terrifying, maybe joyful. You may depart this life fighting, surrendering, crying, or smiling. But you will depart. The journey is yours and yours alone.

There is an end to loneliness, although it may not be at the end of the road you are presently taking. It always lies along the road less taken. The path is uneven and sometimes stony, but the vistas are incredible. You may even discover you will miss some of the loneliness when it is gone.

8

Some Suggested Tools of Change

Form a Loneliness Loves Company Club

> "Desperate times call for desperate measures."
> — Hippocrates

Here is a template of an announcement that you could use, as is, or tweak it to your preference:

"We have formed a group called Loneliness Loves Company. We accept that loneliness is a serious situation. But not so serious that we will allow ourselves to be held hostage by it. We may not love being lonely, but we may come to love being lonely together. Loneliness loves company.

Each week, we extend people the opportunity to check in with each other, while respecting that silence is always an option. There may be discussion; listening to music; viewing a film, video, or photographs; field trips; journaling; and guided meditation. This is not a specifically religious or psychotherapy group. It is a fellowship. Confidentially is expected. All are welcome."

You may wish to discreetly mention this announcement to your friends, church members, women's group, survivor's group, or other interested people. You could also start with the following suggested tool, and then form a group afterward from those who participate.

Listening to the Loneliest Songs In The World

Find one song about loneliness that really speaks to you. You may already know what that song is or you may not.

While you may fear that listening to songs about loneliness will make you even more lonely, these songs might give voice to what you are not able to express. You may even find comfort in hearing someone reflect your inner thoughts and feelings.

These songs can offer you great solace, comfort, and solidarity when listened to alone. You can be alone, lonely, and together with kindred lonely spirits. There is, however, great advantage in taking this a step further by doing this with a group. If you belong to a church or other house of faith and worship, or to a support group, I suggest you form a group around the subject of loneliness. Or it could be a group gathering to process loss and grief. It could also be a group that loves music, and this group could provide yet another category of music to enjoy.

After you convene a group, make some brief introductory remarks, allow people to briefly introduce themselves, and distribute a list of loneliness songs. Encourage them to listen to all the songs on the list so they will be familiar with the song choices. Before they leave, also let them know that when they return, they do not have to talk about themselves unless they choose to. Not

Photographing Loneliness

Meet with the group and discuss the saying, "a picture is worth a thousand words." Ask them if that has ever been true for them. Where have they seen a picture worth a thousand words? Can they describe it to the group?

If people cannot find a time to meet together, disperse to take photos and then regroup to discuss them. Then let them take pictures of loneliness by themselves when they are able and return to the group a week or so later to show or talk about them.

The photos can be taken with a cellphone or camera. Printing them would be good, if possible. If they cannot print the photos or do not have a camera, they could cut loneliness pictures from a publication.

The pictures can be taken anywhere because loneliness is everywhere. A picture is worth a thousand words. When your group gets together after this field trip, pass the photos around. That takes pressure off of participants to talk. The pictures will do the talking.

Going to a Museum Alone

This exercise may begin in loneliness but end in bonds formed between the persons who regather afterward to process the experiences they had while going to a museum alone.

I recently went to the Whitney Museum in New York City to see the exhibit "Edward Hopper's New York." Loneliness is a prominent part of many of his paintings. There are very few people in his paintings and none of them are facing or interacting with each other. All of the reviews of the exhibit mention loneliness although the word never appeared in promotion of the exhibit. In the comments I overheard, many people viewing the paintings specifically mentioned loneliness. The museum was packed with people viewing paintings in which loneliness was a prominent and yet unspecified theme.

I read in Ernest Hemingway's *A Moveable Feast* about him being hungry while viewing a painting by Cézanne. The painting seemed clearer and sharper on his empty belly, causing Hemingway to wonder if the painter was hungry while painting it. Hemingway's hunger connected him more fully to himself, the painting, and the painter.

I was inspired by this to visit the Metropolitan Museum of Art in Manhattan alone and lonely. I was also clear, sharp, perceptive, and alert. Like hunger, loneliness can clarify and sharpen many experiences. Loneliness is a form of hunger.

Many times, in many countries, in many museums, I have found profound intimacy with paintings, painters, hunger, and loneliness. The painter and I may not have lived in the same century or spoken the same language, but we have shared the same hunger and loneliness. Through them we share the same spiritual condition. I wanted to meet the painters and the people in their paintings to discuss what they were feeling while they were painting. I left the museum far lonelier than I had entered it.

I suggest a fasting group of people go to a museum together and once inside, scatter as individuals, and gather after a few hours to share their insights and revelations. They could discuss whether they felt lonely by not having someone to talk to about what they were seeing and experiencing.

You might ask if they noticed other museumgoers more closely than they would have if they were with others from their group. Many may not have gone to a museum alone before. Would they do it again without a group to reunite with? This experience affords them time to be alone as well as time to connect with others who were also alone. Alone together.

Exploring Three Ways of Dining Alone

Dining alone is a luxury afforded to those creative enough in their aloneness and in their loneliness to savor the gift of delicious, nutritious flavors and nutrients that your body will transform into energy to feed your soul. You need not tell anyone you know that dining alone can be a comfort in a noisy and shattered world. When you enter the realm of possibilities known as Dining Alone, just softly say in a centered way "Table for one, please!" And smile.

Knowing that your group has agreed to dine alone at some point during the week and will reconvene at some designated point to discuss the experience can help mitigate the loneliness you may otherwise fear.

At the Botin

I prepared to dine alone at Botin, the oldest restaurant in continuous operation in the world, located in Madrid, Spain. Founded in 1725 and open ever since, this famous destination for diners is mentioned in Ernest Hemingway's *The Sun Also Rises*.

I called the restaurant for a reservation. "How may persons in your party?" I answered, "One." The only reservation I could get was in the distant future on a weekday between the lunch and dinner seatings. I took it, grateful for any opportunity at all. I was seated at a tiny and wobbly table near the doors to the restroom and kitchen and across from a table of eight people enjoying pitchers of sangria, food, and each other. I was clearly seated there for one reason: I was alone.

I could have requested a better table, but why? Lobbying for a better table as a single person is a battle I rarely choose to initiate. I understand that solo diners occupy a table that would be twice as profitable if two persons were seated at it. Solo diners are often presumed to be lonely and that even if they are not, the mere possibility of it is enough to keep an establishment from placing the lonely countenance of a single person at a table near the front door. Solo diners are presumed guilty of loneliness and are silently sentenced to exile in an area that, when I was a maître d'hôtel in Manhattan, we referred to as "Siberia" where they join the likes of people with young children and stragglers without a reservation.

Couples don't like to be seated near solo diners. They are about as happy to see a solo diner seated next to them as they are happy to see someone with a whiny toddler. Proximity to a solo supper eater might put the kibosh on a couple's laughter and intimate conversations. Solo diners are not known to break into laughter.

Dining alone is frequently perceived to be less preferable than dining with others. There are legitimate reasons for this. People do like to talk about the meal they are enjoying. They also talk so much during dinner that they sometimes fail to appreciate the meal. A business lunch, to me, is a bad idea. Conduct the business first, and then go have lunch.

However, dining alone can be quite a spiritual experience, a silent and peaceful sabbatical from a noisy and hectic day. And yet many people don't like doing it. However, you don't need to add people at your table. What needs to change may not be the discrimination and bias against solo diners exhibited by restaurants and other businesses. Your attitude toward dining alone may be what needs to change.

When nothing stands between you and that forkful of food then each bite is a companion to be paid attention to and welcomed inside you that gives you the sensation of completeness.

A lonely meal is not for thinking, talking over, or sharing food. It is just for you. Loneliness is a spice of life. If you show up for yourself in this meal, you are in communion with yourself. There is no emptiness, no craving, no other place to be, no longing or regret in this centeredness. There is only now.

A Simple and Slow Silent Soup Supper Alone with Others

Once a year for several years, I hosted a "Simple and Slow Silent Soup Supper" at which fifty people gathered at one rectangular table, with all the seats only on the outside of the rectangle, facing the center. Each setting had a votive candle, silverware, and a napkin. A few matchboxes were on the table.

People are encouraged not to sit with the person they arrived with or any other person with whom they have ever associated. They are asked to remain silent upon arrival in the area adjacent to the dining room until all are present. Silence begins upon arrival, not upon the commencement of the supper. They are asked to silence their cellphones.

When all guests are present, a member of the dinner team says, "Come, for all things are ready." The people are then seated. A server picks up a matchbook and lights one votive candle. With a gesture, the server invites the other persons to light their own candle. In a moment, there are fifty lit candles in from of each of the fifty silent people.

In the open space at the center of the rectangular table is a serving table, about the size of a card table. The servers are instructed in advance of the supper that it is easy to go too fast, but they can ever go too slow. Slow, silent, and simple service at the supper must be practiced:

- ❀ The servers slowly and silently bring baskets of a combination of flat breads, crackers, and rolls to the center table and strategically distribute them.

- ❀ Servers place pitchers (or bottles) of juice or wine on the center table. They take a pitcher or bottle to the table and pour silently and slowly into each person's glass.

- ❀ A large terrine of soup is brought to the center table along with stacks of bowls (ceramic, not paper). Each portion is ladled by a server into a bowl, and the bowls are carried, one by one, to each diner.

- ❀ This is a contemplative meal, slowly served and silently eaten. The only sounds are the occasional clink of a soup spoon against a bowl, the snap of a cracker, juice being poured from a pitcher to a glass.

- ❀ When the main part of the meal has been served and eaten, the servers bring, one-by-one, a small dish of an individual-size portion of a simple dessert, such as dried fruits and nuts or an individual portion of some other sweet.

❀ After the meal, the servers silently remove the glassware, silverware, bread baskets, and bowls.

❀ We depart in silence.

The diners at first seem self-conscious, uncertain, and a bit nervous. Several glance at their watches. Some try to find a single place to fix their stare, as if the encroaching intimacy is unbearable. There seems to be no purpose, no agenda, no soundtrack, no entertainment, no finale. They are correct in that. Not all people seem fully present.

The Simple and Slow Silent Soup Supper guests find themselves alone together, and together alone. Seated as they are, with everyone facing everyone else in silent solidarity, community is formed. Instead of focusing primarily on people's words, people look at each other. A communal experience feels quite personal. The sound of silence migrates from awkwardness to consolation. Loneliness fades when the art of being alone and in good company with yourself arises. Dining alone can be blissful.

Jesus instructed the disciples to "remember me" in the sharing of bread and wine. He could have said remember me by creating a statue, painting a painting, or performing a dance. However, he chose to be remembered in the sharing these simple, basic elements and, through them, the transformation of "me" into "we."

No law says we must break bread together. We can also break bread alone in communion with God, life itself, or Mother Nature that created the ingredients from which the bread is created. Breaking bread while dining alone may seem to be the violation of a primal need to be together with others. Even the Bible says it is not good for us to be alone (Genesis 2:18).

The prejudice against dining alone exists from the dining room to the mess hall to the banquet hall. Business deals are celebrated over a meal. Thanks and giving are celebrated at communal feasts. Brunches follow baptisms. Banquets follow weddings. And this is good! But we also know that loneliness, if we were to look, is at all these occasions.

Breaking bread is both a ritual and a symbol of belonging. But it can be a symbol of stopping the power loneliness has over you. What is broken open is the potential to be transformed by acceptance that what was once a symbol of loneliness has become a symbol of promise that no one, ultimately, is ever alone.

Dining with a Deceased or Otherwise Departed Person

Sometimes, when eating alone in a restaurant, I feel the spiritual presence of a departed loved one. "Thanks for joining me," I say silently to them. The server starts to remove the place setting on the opposite side of the table and I ask them not to. I do not question the spiritual presence of my departed loved one. I have found that if I am afraid or do not believe, the visits happen less and less frequently. The more open I am to such visits, the more they happen.

I believe the spirit of the person really is there but that, like the disciples on the Road to Emmaus, we are so caught up in anger, grief, and distractions we fail to notice their presence even if we have been praying for it. Paying attention is a prerequisite for just about everything.

Once I am confident the spirit of my loved one is present and it is not just my wishful thinking, I invite the departed loved one to fill the empty chair just as I would welcome anyone else. Their presence is warm, pulsing, and undeniable. Sometimes we have a conversation of the "still, small voice" variety. But I am certain of its authenticity because I am aware that I am not the source of the thoughts, insights, and feelings being exchanged. I silently both listen to and talk to my loved one. When this visitation from a departed loved one happens at home, I speak out loud.

One time my departed six-year-old daughter, Maya, came to me in a restaurant. She appeared to me to be the age she would be now, not the age she was when she died. At one point, I began to withdraw into myself because the pain of missing her was growing even though her spirit was still with me. I became greedy and wanted her physical presence as well as her spiritual presence. As I felt her presence but saw only an empty chair across the table, I began to lose my belief in what was happening. As I began to withdraw, she began to withdraw also.

At these times, I banish all thought and judgement. It is like "being in the zone" described by athletes and many others. If you find yourself thinking, it is essentially over. A Bible story comes to mind. Peter was in a boat with Jesus and, at Jesus's instruction, Peter began to walk on water as had Jesus until he doubted, got distracted, and sank.

I needed to be fully present for my daughter to be fully present. She was there as much as I until we were together no more. When her presence departed, I asked for the check and left the restaurant. There was no doubt it had happened, and there was no doubt when it was over.

These visits are rare, unpredictable, and not contingent upon anything I say or do. They are sometimes painful, but always beautiful. My daughter's death was the most painful thing I have ever experienced. In her absence, I became profoundly lonely. The lonelier I felt, the closer I felt to her. It was my loneliness that was the strongest bond I had with what remained of her. I feared that losing my loneliness would mean losing her. I was stuck. I could not rid myself of the loneliness because it was that very thing that kept me close to what I did not want to lose.

Then I realized my loneliness was an invitation to her. It was my loneliness that beckoned her. In my loneliness, brokenness, and vulnerability, I was the most open to a visitation of the spirit.

Picnicking Alone

My daughter, Celeste, called me one afternoon, shortly after she had moved to a new city. She was alone on a blanket with a sandwich and a bottle of water in a park on a Saturday. She was lonely and I was lonely for her.

I wanted to protect her from her loneliness. What I did instead was to talk with her. I asked her to describe what she was seeing in the park. As she did so, we both began to recognize and appreciate the beauty and peace in the park in her lonely, spiritually heightened, emotionally charged, wide-awake-and-aware way.

Had it not been for loneliness, she probably would not have called me. If it had not been for my loneliness, I might not have been fully present. A father and daughter bonded by loneliness and a thousand miles apart found themselves very much together.

Without loneliness she might have been mindlessly eating a mediocre sandwich rather than savoring every solitary bite as the smell of grass, fresh air, cheese, bread, sweat, and fading perfume all entered her nose and her mind at the same time.

Had it not been for loneliness, I would not be reliving that precious day, as she stayed with her loneliness and I stayed with mine, and the world was suddenly transformed into a garden of splendid delight.

As we revealed our loneliness to each other, nature revealed her loneliness to us.

If it takes being lonely in a park with a mediocre sandwich and a longing for someone to share it with; if it takes all that to see and experience beauty all around and within you; then so be it. My daughter took another bite of her loneliness sandwich. She described the sandwich to me. I could almost taste it. I asked her to savor every morsel. Then I asked her to savor every morsel of loneliness because it too would soon be gone.

My daughter is now married with three children and a needy dog. I bet she sometimes longs for a lovely picnic alone. Near where I live there is a boardwalk over a wetland that leads to a bench overlooking a river. Sometimes I take someone there to show them my sacred place.

Other times I bring a soggy sandwich, a bottle of water, and a slightly bruised apple and go to the bench overlooking a river, alone. I could care less if I am lonely, tired, grumpy, or whatever other human experience is jostling me about at that particular moment.

I sit, close my eyes, and let my thoughts fall like dust particles onto the wetland. Then I open my eyes and slowly unwrap my sandwich. I politely nod my head at the bird on the railing watching me. After unscrewing the lid of my water bottle, I say a prayer of gratitude. An egret flies so low over my head I hear the whoosh of air created by a single flap of its wings as it lands where it always does each time we happen to be there at the same time. Then I smile and enjoy my lunch rendezvous with God and all of God's creation that cares to join us. I feel anything but lonely.

Dancing Alone

A woman and her spouse retired and moved to Florida where they shared many good friends and joyful times. They were active in our church and at their retirement community until her husband died after a brief illness. It was then, according to her, that loneliness became her constant companion.

I met with her about a month after his death. She told me each Saturday night that she and her husband used to dress up and dance in their living room to their favorite songs. When he died, she continued the tradition. She would dress up, play their favorite songs, and dance around the living room. But now she was dancing with herself.

She felt very close to his spirit on those Saturday nights. Dancing alone was actually fun. She could twirl and sway in ways that she could not always do with him when he was still alive. Even though she was dancing alone, she felt confident his spirit was encouraging her to keep dancing. Through dance, she thought, his memory and spiritual presence would remain. As long as she kept dancing.

After a few weeks, that feeling of intimacy with her departed husband began to fade. Dancing alone just was not the same. It began to create more sadness than joy. A few more weeks later, she continued to listen to their music, but no longer danced to it. Eventually, she no longer listened to it either. Loneliness returned and, at first, she became depressed. As we sat in my office, she told me she no longer felt the need to dance alone. She now believes there is sacredness, serenity, and dignity in letting go of what is simply no longer meant to be. Although she and her husband no longer dance cheek-to-cheek, they will be dancing forever soul-to-soul.

In 1991, I convinced a friend to go with me to Dick Shea's Barefoot Ballroom in New York City. We walked up to the second floor where we paid a moderate admission and were immediately asked to check our shoes to protect the wood floors.

The recorded dance music of many genres had one thing in common: to get you on the dance floor in your bare or stockinged feet. Some people danced in pairs, others in small groups that dissolved and reformed with various people who wanted to join. Many people danced by themselves in the floor-to-ceiling glass-walled room. They were their own partner.

Shea's Barefoot Ballroom was frequented by yoga practitioners, aerobics instructors, dance students, and other people who love to dance, but not, at least for that night, in an atmosphere of drinking and prowling for a mate or a date. Some people, I imagine, go there alone simply because they see no reason to stay home.

This experience showed me how being alone does not mean being excluded from activities that many people assume are meant for couples only. What a joy it was just to know that the barefoot ballroom was there as an option.

The Barefoot Ballroom provided a sense of safety and fun for a couple of hours. In my loneliness I found a community of sorts: a community of loneliness that allowed me to be in the presence of others without being prodded into interacting with them. It felt like church to me. At least what I imagined church could be: transformation and transcendence based upon acceptance.

No matter how positive a spin we place on it, loneliness is not always transformed into something beautiful. And yet, even in such situations, there is beauty to be found in accepting and moving on.

Vacationing Alone

Vacationing alone is not only for the lonely. It can be a gift to yourself, a time away from the demands of family, work, and endless duties that slowly pull you away from what you dream of doing.

A vacation alone can be as brief as a weekend or a few hours away from home. It can be to an exotic land where you don't know the language, or to a secluded island where you don't need the language. It can be to a city or a desert, an ocean or a mountain, a place to get active or get lazy. Your choice.

Planning a trip around a theme or a learning opportunity is a great way to be alone while also being in proximity with others. Trips that focus on learning a language through food and culture can be a lot of fun. Many retreat centers and monasteries have solo stays for guided silence, yoga, and mindful nature walks. Trips that assist disadvantaged people are helpful and meaningful.

However, be cautious about finding people, places, and things that result in you being immersed in group activities that camouflage certain feelings and divert you from the many benefits of traveling alone.

Writing Five Letters

Not everyone is a writer. Staring at a blank piece of paper or computer screen may be a lonely experience in and of itself. Wait patiently until the spirit of the one to whom you are writing shows up.

There are a few letters to be written in this exercise. Do not look at all the suggested letters before you write the first one. If this approach doesn't work out, then write thoughts or feelings without worrying about complete sentences. These thoughts and feelings could come in the form of memories, smells, occasions, places… anything. The thoughts and feelings do not need to make sense. There is no correct answer. No one is judging your faith, attitude, or writing skills.

A Letter from You to Me

Sit in a comfortable space, take a pen or computer and write a letter. Make believe this letter is written *to* you by the person for whom you are lonely. Hopefully, this can be a tender and loving letter from the one you miss. Later may come a time for tearful, fearful words. But for now, conjure sweetness, kindness, and compassion as you emotionally and spiritually connect with the one you love and miss.

A Letter from Me to You

Write a letter back *to* the person above. Begin simply, "Hello, I am so pleased that you wrote to me. I am so lonely for you right now…" Then respond directly to the letter you received. Add any thoughts and feelings that come up. You will now have two letters. The first was written to you by the person for whom you are lonely. The second written by you back to that person.

A Letter from Now to Then

This letter is not to or from a person but to a bygone era of your life. Begin this letter with something like, "Dear Days of Old, This is the ___(your present age here)____ year old ____(your name here)____ and I am writing to tell you how much I miss you." Then write, for example, about being lonely for your youth with all the sense of promise, hope, health, and vigor.

Perhaps write about being lonely for a time when your children were young, your church was vibrant and thriving, and neighbors knew each other. Or you can write about being lonely for a better yesterday when politics was not so nasty and elected officials were less self-serving. You could even write a letter to something like a missing ethical and moral world.

A Letter from God to You

In the Book of Exodus, God wrote with his finger on stone tablets and gave them to Moses. If God walks with me and talks with me "In the Garden" (a popular hymn), and if God holds me in the palm of God's hand (Isaiah 49:16 and Ecclesiastes 9:1) and if God speaks through prophets, poets, paupers, priests, and Mother Nature, then why would God not speak to you through a letter, email, or text?

Write a letter from God to you. What does God have to say about your present situation and your loneliness? And what might you say to others also living with loneliness?

A Letter from You to God

Now you know something about what God wants you to know about you and your loneliness. But what do you want God to know?

Do you want God to know you have received more than your fair share of loneliness? Does God need to know you fear there is no way out of loneliness? Now write that letter. Let 'er rip! God has broad shoulders.

Do not destroy these letters. You can look back some day to see what your mind and heart were up to on the day you wrote the letters. And some day you might wish to share one of your letters with someone else or distribute them anonymously in a group to which you belong. Your writings may be a source of comfort and help to those struggling with many of the same things as you.

Write a Loneliness Gratitude List

It is difficult to be resentful and grateful at the same time, but not to be lonely and grateful at the same time. Loneliness can even be heightened by gratitude for a person or group of persons in your life for whom you are lonely. Writing a gratitude list may bring you emotionally and spiritually closer to the object of your affection.

I had a very difficult relationship with my parents, detailed in my book *Forgiving Our Parents*. Part of my process of forgiveness involved writing a gratitude list. It was not easy to do. But doing so helped me realize there were strengths, talents, and resilience born out of the cauldron of difficulty in which I was raised.

That realization allowed me to grieve what was missing, realize what had been gained, and become free to change and move on. Forgiveness and loneliness have at least one thing in common: creating a gratitude list affected the way I perceived things. Gratitude was like the oil placed on the rusty joints of the Tin Man. My body, mind, and spirit could move more fluidly. To get this process moving, I offer the following items from my Loneliness Gratitude List. I Am Grateful to Loneliness for:

- ❀ Keeping me real
- ❀ Being my teacher
- ❀ Inspiring me with visions of wholeness
- ❀ Teaching me compassion for others
- ❀ Opening avenues of creative expression

Begin your gratitude list now, then read it aloud to yourself.

Choosing Your Perceptions

Our perceptions largely form our beliefs and actions. We act, react, and respond as if perceptions are inevitable or preordained. However, it's important to realize we choose our perceptions.

There are many reasons why we perceive things the way we do. Perceptions are based on experience, tradition, personal or cultural stereotypes and prejudice, and recent events in the news. Some perceptions come from religious or philosophical conviction or whether we trust the person with whom we are interacting. Our chosen perceptions sometimes override evidence. We cannot choose perceptions for other people and they cannot choose ours.

When we cease judging, denying, resenting, condemning, and trying to control the perceptions of other people, we move closer to the place where transformation can happen. We cannot always change people, places, and things. But we can change our perceptions for ourselves.

What does this have to do with loneliness? We may choose a perception that people want to keep their distance from us if they sense that we are lonely because lonely people are needy. So, we pretend we are not lonely based on a potentially incorrect perception. We may also choose a perception that someone else is also quite lonely and we should keep our distance from them. But our perceptions are not reality.

We can change our perceptions of loneliness as something inherently negative that may cause people to keep their loneliness a secret. When we nurture the healing of our perceptions, our relationships often take care of themselves. We may be as little as one shift in perception away from freedom.

Balancing Expectations

A lot of our exploration involves expectations of what will happen to us and others when we encounter loneliness. Many of us have been told many times that we expect too much. Others of us have been told that we don't deserve to expect anything. Many of us have given up having expectations because we are so used to being disappointed.

Expectations remain a huge part of our lives, whether we are conscious of them or not. If we could adjust our expectations of how we feel we and others are supposed to behave and believe, we could save ourselves a lot of grief. If we could be more realistic about how people are and what they are capable of, we would have done much of our work on loneliness.

It is not always easy, but when you allow yourself to be yourself then you are able to be more comfortable with who you are. We tend to focus so much on being a partner to one person, a parent to another, an employee to yet another, and so on. We often conform and contort ourselves into what we expect others want us to be that we risk losing track of a more authentic version of ourselves that resides at the core of our being. You may then be able to open up and confide in others what is going on inside of you and reveal some of the issues bothering you without expectations of how you will be perceived.

Take a few moments to think of a person or situation (including yourself) contributing to your loneliness. Don't try to be rational, fair, or convincing. Just allow your expectations to surface. Write one to three things that first come to mind:

❀

❀

❀

Pause a moment, read what you have written, and then write one to three things that you wish or expect to change with that person or situation causing your loneliness:

❀

❀

❀

If you believe your loneliness will never change no matter what you think or do, then write a few lines about why you believe the loneliness will never change:

❈

❈

❈

Now look at what you have written and divide the people, places, and situations into two categories. One is what you wrote about yourself, and the other is what you wrote about others. If you wrote: "If I could get over this shyness, then I will be able to meet someone and be less lonely," that would go in the Myself column. If you wrote "If my child would stop drinking so much, they would have more friends and be less lonely," then that would go in the Others column.

Myself:

❈

❈

❈

Others:

❈

❈

❈

The last part is to take those lists of expectations for yourself and others and divide them into two categories: realistic and unrealistic. For example, you may expect that if your child were to stop drinking, they would have more friends. That might be unrealistic. You may wish it were true. It might be great if it were true. It might, however, be an unrealistic expectation that an end to loneliness will result in an end to drinking.

Now look at each thing you wrote. Be as open and honest as you can be and divide expectations for yourself and others into these two categories. If you cannot decide which category something belongs, place it in both.

Expectations for Myself

Realistic:

❀

❀

❀

Unrealistic:

❀

❀

❀

Expectations for Others

Realistic:

❀

❀

❀

Unrealistic:

❖

❖

❖

When feeling lonely, we sometimes blame others for what we have done to ourselves, and blame ourselves for what others have done to us. It's possible to confuse problems with solutions. For example, we act as if we believe the fear of getting hurt is best remedied by self-imposed isolation. We mistake sadness for self-pity. It then becomes too easy to blame ourselves for being lonely at a party when it is possible that we are not the only one there experiencing the same thing.

However, when we can see what our expectations are then we can begin to clearly see where we are, where we are headed, and if we want to go there. Otherwise, we may stumble through our lonely lives merely avoiding as much pain as possible. We deserve better than that. Knowing what is unrealistic helps us to avoid burnout and maintain the realistic expectation of hope and grace.

Blaming Ourselves, Blaming Others

Self-Blame

Often, we blame ourselves for our loneliness. We may believe loneliness is a result of doing something wrong or bad. We make self-directed judgments such as, "Any fool should know that loneliness would be the outcome of that!" Sometimes it makes us angry or bitter that we are lonely. So we blame ourselves for having these feelings.

Anger and blame directed against ourselves for being lonely is self-victimization and self-punishment. We may blame ourselves for what went wrong in our relationships. Blame makes perfect sense in a society that is over-reliant on logic and cause-and-effect thinking that goes like this:

- ❀ I am lonely and it is painful.
- ❀ I must find the cause of the loneliness and eliminate it.
- ❀ Once I find the cause and eliminate it, I will no longer be lonely.

This fixation on logic, rationality, and cause-and-effect thinking is flawed. Rather than taking ownership of our loneliness, we hunt down the cause of our discomfort and then blame the person, institution, group, political party, or whatever else we hold responsible. The list of blameworthy culprits can include ourselves.

Sometimes things happen simply because they happen. Sometimes what happens is not all about us and what we did and did not say or do. We aren't that powerful. This perpetual need to have an explanation shows our desire to control. We fear randomness and meaninglessness. Blaming ourself or others gives us, temporarily, a sense of safety. "Ah, now I know why I am the way I am," is like a drug, the effects of which eventually wear off. And then we are back to being lonely.

This can also happen to congregations and clergy that seek what or who to blame for their problems and then try to root it or them out. The church may be feeling unwelcome change. Causality thinking goes something like this: Things aren't going as well as they used to. We lack money and members. We must find the cause, the reason. The pastor is clearly not up-to-snuff. If we fire the pastor who is to blame for all they did and failed to do, then we will feel better.

The pastor might even agree with their decision. The payoff for self-blame is a sense of control. If I am powerful enough to have caused the problem, then I just might be powerful enough to stop it. If not, then I only have myself to blame.

Self-blaming people—in an attempt to get out from under the weight of their self-judgment, pain, and loneliness—sometimes try to strike deals with God, such as a clergyperson might do by declaring to themselves and to God, "I will resign if that will stop the angst of the congregation and the curse of my loneliness."

When you blame yourself, you find a reason for everything bad that happens. Then you can try to control your own and other people's behavior so that it won't happen again.

Lonely people often silently try to cure loneliness with isolation. If you do not have such tendencies in yourself, then have mercy and compassion when you recognize them in others. If you do see such tendencies in yourself, realize you alone did not cause loneliness. So you alone cannot cure loneliness. You alone cannot control loneliness. But you alone can accept it. Blaming yourself for loneliness is like blaming yourself for being a sensitive soul. A lonely, sensitive soul is a blessing because it is vulnerable to healing and transformation.

Blaming Others

Don't rid yourself of self-blame by blaming others. We can blame God, fate, genes, lovers, church, COVID-19, or other people, places, and things for our loneliness. But we run the risk of making ourselves perpetual victims.

Blaming others avoids taking responsibility for your part in the problem and your part in the solution. In this blame game, each person claims the only way to break a stalemate is for the other person to change. This could result in never fully accepting loneliness and never being able to transition out of it. How many people do you know (including yourself) who are still angry or depressed years later at the person, thing, or event they believed created loneliness?

Perhaps they hold on to blame, anger, and loneliness because it still makes them feel close. Anger, blame, and loneliness can feel very intimate. Holding on to loneliness means never really having to let go.

Blame is often an attempt, consciously or unconsciously, to get someone else to feel responsible for our feelings. We say things like, "If it wasn't for you, I wouldn't feel lonely." When we stop blaming ourselves and each other, we can truly begin to respond to our own and each other's needs.

Tools of Change Related to Perceptions, Expectations, and Blame

❀ Let go of a belief that you *are* lonely. You may be experiencing loneliness. But loneliness does not define you.

❀ Admit that the events and feelings involving your loneliness really happened.

❀ Accept that the past cannot be undone. There is no hope for a better yesterday. But there is hope for tomorrow.

❀ Be here now. In the present moment, there is no loneliness. Loneliness takes us out of the here and now and into the there and then.

❀ We are not dependent on anyone else to rescue us from our loneliness.

❀ Choose perceptions and balance expectations of how others will or should respond to our loneliness.

❀ Accept ourselves and others for who we and they are rather than who we wish ourselves and them to be.

❀ Accept that people were not born to make us lonely or to save us from it.

❀ Isolation is not a healthy way to treat loneliness. Being in the presence of other lonely people can be a blessing.

- ❀ Loneliness and solitude aren't the same.
- ❀ Talk about your loneliness and issues related to it when they come up, before they become pent-up emotions and attitudes to sort through.
- ❀ Find a clergy member, therapist, sponsor, mentor, or friend to talk to.
- ❀ Listening is vital. People are trying to tell you who they are and who they perceive you to be. Do not prepare rebuttals while they are speaking. Listen deeply. Good listeners are valuable and rare.
- ❀ Learn not to take everything personally. This will only drive you into retreat, isolation, and loneliness.
- ❀ Alcohol and self-prescribed medications do not cure loneliness.
- ❀ Seek the counsel of a physician if you or others are concerned about the depth of your loneliness. Loneliness sometimes masks other serious issues.
- ❀ Do not wound the healers who have come to heal your wounds.
- ❀ Learn the basic tenets of powerlessness over people, places, and things.
- ❀ Lonely people need and deserve healthy foods.
- ❀ Turn to your higher self, higher power, or to God in your prayers, meditations, and visualizations.

Potluck Proverbs

When loneliness has more influence over you that it should, turn to a few proverbs:

- ❀ To make a friend, be a friend.
- ❀ It is easier to act your way into new thinking than to think your way into new actions.

❈ Move a muscle, change a thought; your body and mind are roommates.

❈ Show how much you care; if necessary, use words.

❈ When loneliness appears, smile at it like a returning friend.

❈ It is better to want what you need than to need what you want.

❈ Shop for spiritual food to feed to your spiritual self.

❈ Changes in gratitude beget changes in attitude.

Practicing the Present of Presence

For purposes of loneliness, begin with thinking of presence as the cessation of needless activity so as to be present in this moment.

At the International Plum Village Community of Engaged Buddhism in France, founded by Thich Nhat Hanh, a bell rings every fifteen minutes. When it rings, all activities stop. You stop if you are at the front desk checking in, peeling a carrot in the kitchen, having a conversation, or journaling alone.

When the bell rings, everyone pauses to stop their doing and thinking and go back to their breathing in and breathing out and connecting with themselves. And they smile. The point is to embrace your feeling with tenderness; whether it is fear, anger or loneliness and to be at home with yourself. When the mindfulness bell rings, people might recite to themselves the poem, "Listen, listen, this wonderful sound that brings me back to my true home."

This true home may mean bringing awareness out of the preoccupations of daily living. Focusing on your breath coaxes you back into your body in the present moment. Being in this present and precious moment precludes loneliness since loneliness is often attached to the past or the future. We believe we will lose something we attained in the past or will fail to get something we need in the future. We fear addressing problems in a relationship. That's because we fear we will lose the relationship if we discover something about it that we cannot tolerate. So we withdraw and feel lonely.

There is an expression "Don't just do something. Sit there!" When we, like hummingbirds, flutter from one flower to another, seeking the sweet nectar of life, we become exhausted. We evade loneliness through constant activity and suddenly the clock has run out on the day. We made it! But to what? A life of seeking or avoiding is not living in the present moment.

There is another kind of presence to consider: being present in the presence of someone other than yourself. Getting out of yourself for a while to help another person lessens your discomfort. Doing unto others as you would have others do unto you, charitable acts, and social justice ministries are cathartic. If you are fully present for them.

You can offer comfort of presence if you sit with someone for a while without saying a word. Just the mere fact that you are there is what they need. They need your presence.

I had an experience at a nursing home where I was visiting a woman from the church. I pushed her in a wheelchair to the day room to have a chat. Across the room was another resident in her wheelchair. She was sitting with her son and daughter-in-law.

None of them spoke the entire time we were there. The resident in her wheelchair was reading a newspaper. Her son was in a chair near her. He was silently scrolling through his cellphone. The woman's daughter-in-law on the other side of the wheelchair was just sitting there, doing nothing.

I wondered why the couple bothered to visit. Couldn't they find something to say to her? Surely their silence only exacerbated the loneliness the woman felt. But then I realized my thoughts were all just my projection, based on my assumptions and expectations of how a visit should be. Maybe their presence was enough. Or in that phase of her life, maybe there just wasn't much that needed to be said. Just being present is sometimes enough.

Their way of being together was actually not significantly different than mine. I have no recollection of what I said to my friend during our visit. It's likely she doesn't remember either. I was fine with our conversation, whatever it was, and so was she. The couple visiting the elderly person next to us appeared to be just fine with their silence.

Being intently, contentedly, mentally, spiritually, and corporeally present for each other, without an agenda or expectations, was enough. If something comes up, it comes up. If it doesn't, it doesn't. When something needs to be said, there is plenty of space for words.

That chance encounter at the nursing home changed me. Whenever I am with someone, I give them the gift of presence and say to myself: "Be here now. Just Be... Here... Now..."

Giving the Gift of Listening

Lonely people are generally not great listeners. This does not mean they are uncaring, but they are often self-absorbed. That is not an indictment. People on a stretcher in an ambulance are also self-absorbed. It makes sense, but it doesn't help loneliness. Finding people to listen to you may help, but people also need to be listened to.

There is sometimes no need to explain or excuse anything. You can stop talking, thinking, fidgeting, and simply listen.

The St. Francis Prayer states that it is better to understand than to be understood. By understanding others, you develop the ability to be understood by them. Then you will begin to understand yourself in new ways. It is ironic that the way to receive help is to help others. But it works.

The same goes with loneliness. If you judge others for being lonely and offer them solutions to their loneliness problem, you will open the gate for them to reciprocate and judge you and offer you solutions to their problems. Who wants that? What helps loneliness is learning to listen to others. And being listened to by others.

Learning to H.A.L.T.

This acronym is useful when feelings of loneliness seem to come out of nowhere.

H.A.L.T. stands for never allowing yourself to get too Hungry, Angry, Lonely, or Tired.

The four components of this acronym are used in Twelve Step fellowships. Getting too hungry can trigger getting angry. Some people get snitty when they are hungry. Feeling lonely can be triggered by being hungry, angry, or tired. Sometimes something as simple as a piece of fruit, a nap, or coming to terms with what is angering you can reduce your loneliness.

Get a Loneliness Accountability Partner

A Loneliness Accountability Partner is a person to talk to, confide in, and check in with. It's someone you do not need to explain, defend, or rationalize loneliness to because they experience it also.

Despite our practices of journaling, contemplation, meditation, prayer, nature walks, and other things, a constant threat to our emotional and spiritual development through such self-appraisal is self-deception. We minimize, rationalize, deny, and fail to see our own role in our life situations. We may be unaware of how far we push painful memories or feelings deep within ourselves, hoping they never rise again. Some of us become masters of repression, presenting one "self" to our family, coworkers, and community while another "self" is lonely as we slowly abandon hope that things will change.

That is why we need a partner in the process. As we become accustomed to our loneliness, it can feel uncomfortable to seek a partner to help us assess where we have been fooling ourselves, as well as to ascertain the favorable aspects of ourselves. Living alone with our thoughts and feelings only takes us so far. It is important to find someone that will maintain confidentiality and be able to hear you with a sense of non-anxious detachment.

People who have an accountability partner find they are not alone. None of us are unique. As it says in Ecclesiastes, "There is nothing new under the sun." Sharing your personal story with a trusted person is the beginning of emerging from the darkness of loneliness.

Eight Steps to Accepting Loneliness

❋ Admit we are lonely and our lives are constrained by it.

❋ Come to believe that a higher power (whom many, but not all, call God) could restore us to wholesomeness.

❋ Decide to turn loneliness over to this higher power.

❋ Make a searching and openminded inventory of loneliness in our lives.

❋ Admit to our higher power, to ourselves, and to at least one other person, the origins, nature, and characteristics of our loneliness.

❋ Became willing and ready to seek and accept help in the transformation of loneliness.

❋ Seek through presence, prayer, meditation, contemplation, and creativity to maintain conscious contact with what has come into focus as a result of our journey with loneliness.

❋ In humble recognition of our having benefitted from this transformation of consciousness, circumstances, creativity, and community, we commit to helping others in their journey toward, with, and beyond loneliness.

A Closer View of Step Four

Shop owners routinely take an inventory of their merchandise. They rarely decide to close shop because not everything is going according to plan. However, they are willing to see what should be kept and what needs to be discounted. The same is true when we take an emotional and spiritual inventory of ourselves. This exercise is similar to a Lenten introspection, a self-appraisal most effective when conducted with an open mind.

To illustrate this point to Sunday School children during Lent, I borrowed cans of food from our food pantry and covered the labels of some with thick paper of various colors. Then I wrote such words as sad, happy, mean, kind, love, hate, and a few other words and intermingled them with regular canned fruits, soups, and vegetables, and had them in a grocery bag.

After taking the cans out of the bag, I asked the kids what should be kept and what should be discarded. I made sure to take lima beans out of the bag first. Then I asked the children if each can should be placed on the top, middle, or lower shelf. The top shelf was for things they thought should be kept and prominently displayed. The middle shelf was where they would place things of which they were uncertain. The bottom shelf was for what should be discarded.

Lima beans, not surprisingly, went on the bottom shelf. Tomato soup was a top-shelf hit. I interspersed actual food items with the cans wrapped with hate, love, glad, sad, mean, kind, and so on.

Some interesting conversations, feelings, and associations came up. For example, anger went on the middle shelf because as the children said, anger is sometimes appropriate and valuable and sometimes not. Hate was strictly bottom shelf. But one child said, "But what if I hate lima beans?"

I pulled out a can of loneliness. The decision to place it on the bottom shelf was unanimous. I asked them if the world would be a better place without loneliness. They paused. The youngest ones nodded yes. I asked if anyone had ever been lonely. Mentions of departed family members (animal and human) were mentioned in soft tones.

Trying hard not to manipulate feelings, I mentioned that if they had never met their departed family members or their pet then they would not have felt loneliness. I then asked if anything good ever came out of loneliness. One mentioned making a phone call. Another would write a poem. Loneliness was moved to the middle shelf.

Perhaps you are willing to take an inventory of yourself. This is not meant to be an exhaustive inventory. It is simply something to get the process of self-assessment moving in your direction. In the box below, write six things about yourself you would like to keep:

1.

2.

3.

4.

5.

6.

Now write six things about yourself that you would like to reduce or discard:

1.

2.

3.

4.

5.

6.

Write six things about yourself that, rightly or wrongly, you believe other people may perceive in you that could be a factor in them staying away from you, or things that may contribute to your loneliness:

1.

2.

3.

4.

5.

6.

We will never live to see the day when loneliness is eradicated. However, we can live to see the day when contributing factors to loneliness that lie within us are lessened or disappear. This discovery, uncovering, and recovery is a profoundly spiritual process, even if it does not feel like it.

Fighting or Fleeing Loneliness

Our instinctual response to pain and tragedy is to protect and defend ourselves by trying to get away. This is the fight or flight response of an involuntary general adaption syndrome.

By trying to run from loneliness, you are actually honoring a response to trauma. You may at first have tried to fight or fend off loneliness. Failing that, you tried to run away. That is a perfectly human, instinctual response. The problem is that by trying to fight or escape, you create a new vulnerability, a new wound. You may flee your lonely self or a lonely relationship by trying to crawl out of it and escape into addictions, an affair, distractions, compulsive cleaning or exercising, worry, anger, numbness. or even church activities, prayer, or leadership.

The irony of seeking to be free of loneliness is that to do so we must first stop fighting it.

Fighting against loneliness makes as little sense as fighting against the color of your eyes. A twelve-step recovery fellowship maintains that people are lonely because they are self-centered. However, self-centeredness does not mean you are selfish. It just means that your point of reference is you, often with little regard for others. This may result in one part of yourself fighting against another part of yourself in a futile battle to end loneliness.

When President John F. Kennedy was shot, his wife, Jackie, tried to crawl out of the limousine. A few reports showed her trying to "run away" and claimed that a good and loving wife would have stayed and not attempted to abandon her husband. As if it was not bad enough to be sitting next to her husband when he was murdered, Jackie Kennedy was being called a bad woman, a bad wife, and a bad person.

Just hours after the assassination, with her husband's blood still on her dress, she stood next to Lyndon Johnson on a plane back to Washington as he was sworn in as the new President of the United States. The First Lady stood there and her mere presence assured the nation that a smooth transition of power between one administration and another was taking place. In the height of that situation, she had two young children waiting for her at home. We know her attention turned to them. Her attention also turned to her country. She knew that how she dealt with her loss and loneliness would influence how we deal with ours. Suddenly, Jackie Kennedy was being called a good woman, a good wife, and a good person.

Which Jackie Kennedy is the one to honor? The one who tried to save herself, or the one who tried to save the country?

Perhaps we should honor both. Love and concern for others is not always possible. Sometimes in our attempts to cope with loneliness and pain, we focus only on ourselves, and sometimes we focus only on others. Both can be necessary. Both can be beneficial. And both can be problematic unless we find balance between them.

And when tragedy struck, she was torn between wanting to stay with her husband in the fight for his and her life and the desire to flee for her life, leaving her husband behind. Fight or flight.

In our relationships with individuals and with institutions such as the church, people experience loneliness. They may become active in church in an effort to end their loneliness. Although they join groups and attend Bible class, loneliness remains.

Sometimes the loneliest people are involved in the most groups. God bless them for their service, but take away their function and they may lapse into feeling useless and lonely. Relationships and activities lessen or cease. Throw in a little aging and an inability to physically get to church and what is left is just you. And they are back at being lonely. And the lonelier they get, the lonelier they remain.

Lonely people, like all people, are part fight and part flight. We want to combat our loneliness and if it doesn't work then we want to flee. It is helpful to understand and accept parts of ourselves that we don't like. We need to come to terms with who we are, and how we react and respond to other people. No one is perfect.

9

A Conclusion of Sorts

I hope *The Gospel of Loneliness* has shown you that loneliness is
a gift.

It may not feel like a gift or be the gift you were hoping for,
but it is a gift, nonetheless. And like any gift, the gift of loneliness is meant to be unwrapped, opened, explored, appreciated,
and utilized. Being lonely means you still yearn, believe, hope,
imagine, dream, and desire.

Loneliness can feel like you are living in the dank darkness
of a basement. To gain release from the power it has over your
life, you need to move to a higher floor, where fresh air and light
grant you a new perspective. This process is virtually impossible

if you focus almost entirely on yourself, your memories, regrets, and resentments.

It is ironic that the way to help yourself is to help others. But it is true. When you find another lonely person to be part of your life and begin to think about how you can be of help and support to them, it is almost impossible not to help yourself.

Loneliness is something you have in common with all people and with God. Blessed loneliness can allow you to see others in yourself and yourself in others. It can enable you to connect with your divine nature and the divine nature in others. The loneliness in me bows reverently to the loneliness in you.

When the student is ready, the teacher appears. Loneliness is a great teacher of vital life lessons such as becoming strong, centered, confident, compassionate, and independent. This kind of person is rarely lonely.

Notes

1.   Paul Tillich, *The Eternal Now* (New York: Scribner, 1963), 17–18.
2.   Rhitu Chatterjee, "Americans Are a Lonely Lot, and Young People Bear the Heaviest Burden," *Shots Health News from NPR*, May 1, 2018, https://www.npr.org/sections/health-shots/2018/05/01/606588504/americans-are-a-lonely-lot-and-young-people-bear-the-heaviest-burden.
3.   Katie Hafner, "Researchers Confront an Epidemic of Loneliness," *New York Times*, September 5, 2016.
4.   Ibid.
5.   Amy Krentzman, Elizabeth A. R. Robinson, Brian E. Perron, and James A. Cranford, "Predictors of Membership in Alcoholics Anonymous in a Sample of Successfully Remitted Alcoholics," *Journal of Psychoactive Drugs* 43, no. 1 (2011): 20–26.

6. Sharon Jayson (Kaiser Health News), "Loneliest Generations: Millennials, Gen Z Sometimes Struggle to Make Connections," *Milwaukee Journal Sentinel*, March 15, 2019.
7. Hafner, "Epidemic of Loneliness."
8. Friedrich Nietzsche, *Thus Spoke Zarathustra*, trans. Adrian del Caro (Cambridge: Cambridge University Press, 2006), 47.
9. Paige Cornwell, "Robot Babies that Schools Use to Discourage Teen Pregnancy May Do Opposite, Study Finds," *Seattle Times*, August 25, 2016.
10. C.G. Jung, *Memories, Dreams, Reflections*, trans. Richard and Clara Winston (New York: Vintage, 1963), 356.
11. Andrew Perrin, "Mobile Technology and Home Broadband 2021," Pew Research Center, June 3, 2021, https://www.pewresearch.org/internet/2021/06/03/mobile-technology-and-home-broadband-2021/.'
12. Natalie Rahhal, "Loneliness Changes the Brain," *Daily Mail*, May 17, 2018, https://www.dailymail.co.uk/health/article-5740883/Loneliness-changes-brain-Isolation-chemical-makes-feel-afraid-aggressive-study-shows.html.